FOR CRYING OUT LOVE

FOR

Transform Suffering

CRYING

Through Gospel Stories

OUT

Prayer and Love

LOVE

TIM KOCHEMS, PHD

This is a work of nonfiction. However, the personal anecdotes and stories within reflect my own memory and experience of the events and people involved. They do not purport to portray others' truths.

Other than my mother, those specifically identified by first and last names, and my wife, Pam, the people in my personal stories are not meant to portray any specific individual person I have known or encountered. Every other portrayal of an individual person is a disguised portrayal and usually a blend of my experiences with friends, people I have encountered, and people with whom I have worked.

There is nothing in this book that should be taken as professional psychological advice meant for a specific reader or advice for a specific personal situation of a reader.

Cover and interior formatting by KUHN Design Group | kuhndesigngroup.com
Copy editor: Elizabeth Sain
Website developer: Kiersten Armstrong | 646.331.3500 | kierstenaa@gmail.com

First edition

ISBN: 979-8-9943954-0-0 (paperback)
ISBN: 979-8-9943954-1-7 (ebook)

Published in the United States of America

Go to www.forcryingoutlove.com for contact and ordering information.

Dedicated to the people who
worked with me in psychotherapy,
shared their suffering and loves with me,
and inspired me
and to those with whom I shared Love.

Two universal…paths of transformation
have been available to every human being God
has created…: great love and great suffering.

RICHARD ROHR, *THE NAKED NOW*

How good of you, God, to make truth
a relationship instead of an idea.

RICHARD ROHR, *THINGS HIDDEN*

When You Can Endure

When the words stop
And you can endure the silence
That reveals your heart's pain
of emptiness
Or that great wrenching-sweet longing,
That is the time to try and listen
To what the Beloved's
Eyes
Most want
To
Say.

HAFIZ (RENDERED BY DANIEL LADINSKY)

CONTENTS

Introduction: Prayer Heals the Way Love Heals 1

PART 1: THE CALL AND RESPONSE OF NATURAL, EXPERIENTIAL, AND RELATIONAL PRAYER

1. The Drowning Followers of Love 15
2. Longing 25
3. Saying "No" to God 33
4. The Anxiety, Heartbreak, and Danger of Human Displacement 41
5. The Families of the Holy Innocents 53
6. The Overwhelmed Young Adult, Age Thirteen to Thirty 63
7. The Suffering Family 69
8. Guilt 83
9. The Help Rejector and the Caregiver 93
10. The Good but Guilty Shepherd 103
11. Systematic Oppression 113
12. Illness and Death Return 123
13. Misogyny 131
14. Our Painful Limitations 141
15. Our Damaged Home 149
16. Group Choices: Hope Falls Toward Despair 157
17. Jesus and His Fellow Revolutionaries 163

18. Despair and Descent 171
19. The Remains of Suffering: Trauma 179

PART 2: DEEPEN PRAYER'S ROOTS WITH AWARENESS, ATTUNEMENT, AND GRATITUDE

20. The Feeling Experience of Prayer: An Analogy Corrected . . 189
21. Be Aware 195
22. Attune 203
23. Be Grateful 207

Conclusion 211
Epilogue 213

Acknowledgments 215
Meet the Author 217

INTRODUCTION

PRAYER HEALS THE WAY LOVE HEALS

This book is full of cries and responses, stories of suffering and love. I find that stories reach out emotionally and call to us, invite us to get involved. Those of us in persistent pain often cry out, the most natural prayer. Others of us, not all and not always, try to respond lovingly. The movement is toward a healing wholeness. Whether in fiction, memoir, or those sparse descriptions of suffering and healing in the Christian Gospels, so many of our most memorable stories come from those spaces where there are cries of suffering and responses of love. I wrote this book to draw us more intimately into our stories of ongoing human vulnerability, our natural responses of prayer, and the healing companionship of Love. The stories are traditional and personal. Hopefully, they will resonate with some of your own, and you'll feel the invitation to share your own in prayer or with others you trust. As you will see, my approach is natural, experiential, and relational. It is oriented to love and in fact engages Love.

Yes, Love is how I refer to and address God. Of course, there is a Christian biblical tradition for this, but my primary reason for doing so is experiential. Early in my life I was attracted to the notion of God and my knowledge of Jesus. Yet, they held little power or commitment until I grounded "God" and even Jesus in my experience of neighborhood walks with my beloved grandfather, my feelings of being held and inspired in nature when camping with my family, and my loving friendships in high school. Since then, I feel most related to the Ultimate Loving Mystery we often refer to as God when I'm engaged in or witnessing loving relationships. That's when I glimpse how God and Jesus work. Profoundly then, I find it impossible to differentiate love and Love working in our lives.

I guess I take after my mother in that way. My dear mother is ninety-eight, living in the tiny Midwestern home I grew up in. She also is in hospice care. One night recently she woke up in some difficulty and cried out. Later, once calm, she asked Sue, the caregiver who was right there lovingly caring for her, "Are you Jesus?"

Though my mom has a significant amount of dementia, I don't think she was confused. I think she just wanted clarity about who was answering her prayer. After all, crying out expecting or just hoping for a loving response is the most natural prayer. Additionally, as I told Sue later, "In that moment, you had the only hands Jesus had to care for my mom." This is what I mean by prayer being natural, experiential, and relational. My mother's experience that night was that her very human, natural prayer, her crying out assuming relationship, was answered. It was answered lovingly within relationship. I think Jesus would be quite happy to have Sue, a beautiful black woman, identified as him by my white mother. While my mother refers to God as Jesus, she seems to have the same difficulty I do with not being able to differentiate Jesus from love.

Of course, not wanting Sue to miss a priceless opportunity, I also suggested she tell her two children that some wise old woman thinks she is Jesus! Shouldn't children know that about their mother?

My experience with my mother affirmed my decision to focus this book on chronic suffering. She has been on the edge of actively dying for three years. That's chronic. In addition, my mother's decline brought together my brothers and me for her care. That's positive, yes, but it also brought the recurrent painful conflicts that come with the three of us being together even for a common cause.

Through my over forty years of experience as a clinical psychologist as well as a psychoanalyst and spiritual director, I became acutely aware that many of our positive stories of people doing good, healing, and helping others often crowd out the stories of people suffering chronically. Love knows it's rare that we get the whole story. Easier parts are left in, more difficult parts are left out. We may get the first terrible reports in the news for a few days, but not what happened next and over the following months or years. Chronic suffering often remains or returns, and it is always difficult to face.

Some seeds are like positive stories. When sown in moist, fertile ground, they germinate immediately and begin to sprout. Many vegetables and common flowers have such seeds. Their seeds make for simple, easy, positive stories that nourish us.

There are other kinds of seeds, however, that don't fit the stories of easy germination. Black-Eyed Susan, Lupine, Milkweed, Redbud, Flowering Dogwoods, and even wheat are some of the beautiful and nourishing plants that have more difficult journeys to sprouting new life. These seeds have evolved protective shells to deal with a range of harsh environmental conditions like extremes of heat, cold, drought, or flooding. Those conditions are what add danger and challenge to the stories of these protected seeds. These seeds take longer and more effort to germinate, to open up. We hear the stories of protected seeds less often. Those stories are more difficult, and they attend more to what goes on under the surface.

The seeds of all our stories expect to find fertile ground in Love. Even as I attend to easy stories that are well grounded and already breaking into the light, I continually find nearby stories of chronic and traumatic suffering trying to sprout new life just below the surface. If those stories don't get the time and attention, the love, they need as part of the whole of life, they'll remain dormant, cut off from the whole, and perhaps die that way. When that happens, everyone misses out on experiencing the whole story of the many ways Love can and does flourish even in the dark.

Chronic suffering greatly influences my approach to prayer and Love. It convinced me that prayer is relationship—a natural, sustained, long-term relationship whether we are conscious of it or not, whether we are religious or not, whether our prayers are answered quickly or directly or not. We all try to take root in and sprout from the continual back-and-forth communication, the call-and-response relationships among ourselves and the loving ground of all being.

In fact, the most important thing I learned about ongoing suffering, prayer, and Love was about relationship, and no one ever told me. I have also never read it in the many books on prayer and spirituality that I have consumed. What I learned over decades from my experience with others and myself was this:

Prayer heals the way love heals.

Everything in this book is meant to lead you to have your own personal experience of this accessible wisdom.

What healing looks like and how it feels will vary. How will you experience it? For some it will be relief from pain and symptoms—to some degree, for some time. For others it will mean more comfort and a greater sense of meaning and participation in life in the midst of ongoing suffering. One word for this greater comfort and meaning is "wholeness," another is simply "love." This is how love heals: Our experience of wholeness and love is greater interconnection within the parts of our individual selves as well as between ourselves and the world. Some say they are more attuned to the whole of themselves, to their most true identity amidst all their other parts and their pain. Others feel more interconnected to other people and the whole of life amidst all its chaotic positive and negative aspects. For all, wholeness or love can decenter pain and suffering, and it can recontextualize or metabolize it in ways that offer significant relief—to some degree, for some time, and sometimes a lot for a long time. Relationships or interconnections are the building blocks of wholeness and love. Prayer is relationship.

Are you familiar with suffering? Directly or indirectly? Especially chronic or traumatic suffering? Have you had any impulse at all to cry out for help? Have you loved or been loved; have you desired love? This book will be useful to you. Useful regardless of your religious tradition, or whether you are a believer, doubter, seeker, or curious. There is nothing dogmatic here. This book will particularly fit you if you attend to and respect your own experience, desire to be deeply known and understood, and long for a world oriented to and engaged with love.

While I refer to and address God as Love, and will do so throughout this book, there is nothing here that requires you to do the same. In fact, my approach to prayer values *your* experience. Trust it. If you feel hurt or disappointed by God, it is important to express your hurt and anger in prayer even without addressing God in any formal way. Just like anyone who is being confronted with anger, I am certain God will know who your anger is directed at, and God can handle it.

If you do not have a way of comfortably naming Ultimate Meaning or the Mystery that we all acknowledge is beyond all names, that is OK. Like me, maybe you have had the experience of getting to know someone before you exchange names. There is no need to direct your prayer by name. I'll repeat over and over again, prayer is relationship. Relationships develop over time. Over time, if needed, you'll learn how to address your prayer. In fact, often, you won't need to address each other in the shared silence between you, sitting in silence or working side by side in silence. There are long traditions of relating to God in silence.

If you do pray with words and images, or would like to try, I encourage you to name the Ultimate Loving Mystery beyond all names in any way that fits your experience and understanding: Spirit, Father, Mother, Jesus, Lord, Krishna, Beauty, Goodness, My Innermost Heart, Truth. At some point, you may be moved to use endearments as you address your prayer: My Dear, My Sweetness, or, as I do often, My Love. Feel free to trust your developing relationship. I hope you will bear with me as I model how I trust my experience and address God as Love.

You'll know over time that you are actually relating, praying, and attuned to Love. The evidence will be noticeable when that relationship leads to more relationships and deeper relationships. Intimacy leads to more intimacy. Love leads to loving. Loving leads to more love. Love leads to healing through wholeness. I hope you will test out these relational truths for yourself.

Think about it, if God communicates with us humans at all, it has to be through all our senses, through our experiences within our world, through our human capacities like our intelligence, our intuition, our imagination, our creativity, and, powerfully, our relationships.

THE FRAME OF THIS BOOK

In each chapter that follows, I begin by naming a kind of chronic suffering that could be familiar to you or someone you love. I also summarize a traditional story from the Christian Gospels. I start with those stories because they are familiar and, though positive, they are easily seen to be at the intersection of suffering, prayer, and Love.

Then, in order to have the story reflect the challenges of chronic suffering that so many people experience, I creatively transform the story by asking questions of it. The basic story is unchanged. Not to worry, I am not about to change a sacred scripture. However, I do ask one or more of three simple questions that you too could learn to ask. The purpose is for you to learn to transform the story for use in your prayer to better fit your actual experience of suffering. We can contextualize your suffering within the relationships of the story. We do this by asking: What led up to this story? What else is happening at the same time? What occurs later? These questions can be asked of any story—personal stories, stories from literature, or stories from any religious tradition.

I am thankful for the simple, positive story of my mother and Sue. My mother cried out, and Sue answered. However, if you were to ask what led up to that moment, I'd tell you about my mom being on the edge of dying for three years. If you asked what else is happening at the same time, I'd share that my brothers and I come together to lovingly care for her and we run into recurring, intense, unresolvable conflicts among us. And, if you asked what occurs later, I'd describe how our suffering continues, AND how Love is continually present and awaits our sharing our experiences within our relationships. I share my story with Love in prayer and within my loving relationships—again, it is difficult to differentiate Love and the loving relationships within my life.

Like with the story of my mother and Sue, the three questions I just listed can be used to open up the chronic suffering just below the surface of most stories. With the Gospels, this is an exercise in imagination. Again, I do not change the Gospels. My intention is to model for your imagination how the Gospel stories could reflect more of your experience. As they do, you can bring more of yourself to your relationship, which is prayer, with Jesus, God, Love, or in silence.

In some of the Gospel stories, for instance, I imagine the answer to the question: What else might have been going on as Jesus cured people? One answer is that there were others who needed or wanted his attention, who needed healing. Did you ever think that Jesus didn't heal everyone? What occurred later? Many he did heal probably suffered again. Do you know his friend Lazarus, the one he brought back from the dead, died again? These are the stories of repetitive suffering, the wounds of the Gospel stories reopened, with a healing purpose.

When suffering is repetitive, prayer needs to be repetitive. The stories in this book invite you to identify and share your chronic suffering within your ongoing relationship with Love. Those of us chronically or traumatically suffering often fall into isolation and despair. If you have suffered chronically or know of someone who has, these transformed stories just might catch and hold you or those you care about, stopping that fall, and maybe freeing you or a friend for something different and more positive, even if only for moments at first. Within each chapter's transformed Gospel story, there is a place for the chronic sufferer with Jesus. Most transformed Gospel stories end by portraying the suffering persons confronting Jesus. In other words, they end in relationship and prayer.

Each chapter also includes a contemporary story from my own personal or professional experience that also addresses the type of chronic suffering portrayed in that chapter.* These stories do not include Jesus as a character, but the suffering is still brought to Love in some way. They also end in relationship and prayer. This book is structured so that you can jump around among the chapters to find the stories that resonate most with your experiences. Most people will resonate with many chapters, and chapter 1 is a good place to begin.

There are long traditions within Christianity of praying with one's imagination and scripture. Both Francis of Assisi and Ignatius of Loyola used imagination by placing themselves in Gospel scenes. I do something similar in each chapter. Within Jewish tradition, midrash is a very old way of interpreting scripture that asks questions of the texts as I do here and reimagines some of the stories in ways that do not replace the originals. Instead, the reimagined stories are offered as ways to be in conversation with the originals, similar to what I do here. Contemporary theologians within most religions also interrogate their sacred scriptures to uncover and develop the stories of people

---

* The situations and people portrayed in the personal and professional stories are not to be identified with any particular actual person, people, or situations. They are disguised conglomerations of actual events and people. The exceptions to this are my wife Pam, my mom and her caregiver Sue, and everyone that I refer to by both first and last names.

who have been overlooked within the mainstream traditions—the stories of women, for example.

Some people, while praying, will place themselves in the transformed Gospel stories and play them out like detailed internal movies with dialogue. Others, and this is one of the ways I pray with these transformed stories, may use them as a way of stirring and focusing the desire to talk with Love about the personal suffering we or those we care about are experiencing. We can also pray in silence: With the stimulation of any transformed Gospel story, we can simply hold a picture in our hearts and minds of Love with us in our specific suffering, companioning us and sitting in silence with us and our suffering.

Every chapter in part 1 leads us to more awareness of our ongoing relationship with Love. Each of these chapters invites us to deepen that relationship consciously by sharing our suffering with Love. The chapters in part 2 describe how to continue to nurture our relationship with Love by increasing our awareness of how Love is present and working in our daily lives, attuning ourselves to Love by actively loving, and always practicing gratitude as we are able.

Everything in this book is meant to lead you to have your own personal experience of this accessible wisdom: Prayer heals the way love heals.

Simply, prayer is loving relationship, and love leads to more love. May it be so for you, all of us, and our world.

IMAGINE AND PONDER

- Have you had experiences where Love and love can't be differentiated? Do you have relationships where Love and love are entangled?

That confusion is a good thing, something to celebrate: It is about relationship and its possibilities; Love alive and active within you, others, and the world.

PART 1

THE CALL AND RESPONSE OF NATURAL, EXPERIENTIAL, AND RELATIONAL PRAYER

Our universe has evolved and continues to evolve toward love, consciousness, and complexity—all interrelated within the whole. So, . . .

- The Ultimate Loving Mystery that is beyond all words and energizes ongoing creation is actively present here and now and waits with love for our responses.
- Praying with suffering is our responding to Love by crying out—sharing and expressing our suffering within our relationship with Love.
- As we evolve, Love responds with presence and compassion—within ourselves, through others, and through our world of nature and happenstance.

CHAPTER 1

THE DROWNING FOLLOWERS OF LOVE

(Jesus Calms the Storm)

Many people came to me over my professional career because they loved much and yet were continually disappointed in the responses they received. The most poignant stories were those of women and men who as adults and even as children tried heroically, over years, to keep afloat some constellation of their difficult, often dysfunctional families. They tried to share joy, support others, and help face challenges. Often their families didn't appreciate their efforts, didn't assist, even devalued and rejected them. All of these people came to me exhausted from trying to navigate through storms that could sink their family's boat and drown them in despair. They took their disappointments personally, often concluding incorrectly that their own human limitations were inadequacies, weaknesses keeping their love from sustaining their families during the storms of life.

Those we love can be quite limited too. Sometimes those we love disappoint us. Sometimes they hurt us. Sometimes our own love doesn't make the difference in others that we desire, through no fault of our own.

The stories in this chapter address what can happen as we orient our lives to do good in our world, as we orient our lives to Love. Being human in limited bodies, integral to the earth with its own limitations, to love anyone or anything is to be more vulnerable. Separation and loss, aloneness, rejection, and being limited to relieve others' pains, even the pains of the earth, these are the sufferings that come with love. The following stories can help us pray with our limitations and the limitations of Love amidst the often-recurring storms of life.

JESUS CALMS THE STORM
(Mark 4:35–41; see also Matthew 8:23)

This well-known Gospel story is about Jesus and some of his followers in a boat in the midst of a dangerous storm at sea. At the end of a long day, he asks them to take him to the other side. Once at sea, as they are fulfilling his request, a violent storm suddenly arises. As it does, their fears rise with it. Surprisingly, Jesus is not just unafraid, he's asleep! His followers are eventually able to wake him and he calms the storm.

The usual moral of this story is simple. Love will protect us. No matter how long the storm. Even if it appears for a while that Love is asleep, the power of Love will eventually calm the storms we find ourselves in. The darkness surrounding us will turn to light. We will come to safe harbor.

LONG-TIME SUFFERING

Most of us, however, at some point in our lives are surprised to learn that doing good, following Love, loving, often does not protect us or those we love from suffering. That kind of suffering can lead to a long-term loss of trust in Love, even despair, or a rageful rejection of Love. If Love often doesn't protect us, it is easy to feel in danger and alone. Life then becomes a quest for protection of one kind or another, not a quest for Love. Worse, nothing can be saved forever, so it seems we all better hold onto whatever we can for as long as we can. If nothing lasts, then how can anything be ultimately meaningful? We fall back on collecting money or possessions, gratifications, obtaining power, winning, fortifying boundaries, isolating, or hiding.

PRAYER

Prayer is relationship with Love. We are vulnerable in every relationship, even our relationship with Love. What would it look like to bring our desire for protection to Love? Our self-blame? Our despair? And what would it feel like to bring directly to Love our disappointment in Love and even our anger at Love? Would we risk sharing these feelings with Love? How might Love respond? The stories that follow illustrate and begin to answer these questions. They offer a model for how you might bring your own suffering to Love.

THE TRANSFORMED STORY

(What else is happening? What occurs later?)

See Jesus call his followers to take him to the other side of the Sea of Galilee. They respond willingly. Additional followers and interested bystanders take to other boats. No one wants to be left behind. No one wants to lose touch with what he seems to call out in them, their goodness, their best selves, a greater wholeness.

Feel free to imagine yourself called by Jesus, and prepare to board the boat that he is in or another boat of people who literally want to follow him. Alternatively, you could place yourself in line for a boat with those who are just curious about him, curious enough to want more of him on this one day.

Imagine the time of day; picture the degree of sunlight, the few white clouds and the sparkling sea. See the rocks along the shore. Feel the breeze, if any, and the chill or heat of the day. Notice the sand or grass or stones around the boats before they are launched.

Place yourself in the story in one of the boats.

You want to do good in some way. Jesus is a model. You don't want to lose touch with him, his spirit, how he loves, his inspiration.

The boats push off. Soon, you pass by fishing boats and, before you know it, you are quite far from shore. Feel the rocking and movement of the boat you are in. Hear the wood creaking, the oars in the water or the wind in the sail, the waves lapping at the sides of the boat. Smell the sea.

As time goes by, feel the wind pick up and the quality of light change. The sun is being covered by quickly forming towering clouds. The clouds become darker each moment. Notice conversation slowing and then stopping. Concern builds.

See the storm forming over the sea and quickly overtaking all of the boats, including the one with Jesus, including the one that you are in. Suddenly, the day has darkened like night. Jesus, everyone else, and you are in the midst of that night. The wind-driven, heavy, cold rain begins. Each moment the storm worsens.

You can't help looking in the direction of Jesus. When your eyes can see through the storm and make him out, Jesus appears … to be sleeping. Jesus sleeps! He called people who cared to answer his call, and he sleeps. He sleeps while his followers, all the varied people on the sea who responded to him, you among them, and others, like those fishing, who are just innocently nearby, become more and more alarmed and afraid for their lives.

You followed him into something much different and more dangerous, more difficult, than you expected. You are disappointed that he is sleeping, and you are afraid. Some people, maybe including you, are angry. People in your own and other boats are trying to observe from a distance how he will respond. He is neither sailor nor fisherman, but in times of danger shouldn't everyone want to be available to help? Shouldn't all hands be on deck? And none of you but the fishermen would be in these boats now if it weren't for him.

Imagine a few of the boats, not the one with Jesus, are swamped and sink, or capsize and break apart in the waves. Imagine chaos. Intense efforts are made to save the people floundering in the sea.

Nevertheless, some people perish.

After the winds and waves are calmed by Jesus, everyone is relieved—to a degree. You eventually come to shore after that challenging ordeal. You and your companions are emotionally and physically exhausted. Perhaps someone you know perished in the storm. Perhaps someone you tried to save slipped from your grasp.

Get accustomed to the land again. Feel some, but not all, of the tension and fear in your body ease. Begin to notice your own feelings regarding these happenings—your exhaustion, certainly. Sadness and grief too. Perhaps rising anger.

Picture Jesus. You and your companions move closer to him. He calmed the storm. He saved lives. But not everyone's. Imagine Jesus hearing the news of the missing people and those who died. He motions for everyone there to come closer. He looks into your eyes with compassion. He wants to hear in your own words what you experienced, what you feel. You begin to express the whole of what you are feeling and your experience.

PRAYER

All of this is prayer. All of it is relationship: Jesus's presence, your curiosity, his call, your responding, following, sharing the devastating storm together, feeling Jesus's saving but also disappointing response, seeing his welcome, coming to him with your experience and acute feelings, and his compassion.

A CONTEMPORARY TRANSFORMATION

It was in 1979 that I first imagined and offered a transformed Gospel story to someone I was working with in psychotherapy. It was this story of Jesus calming the storm. I offered it to Linda, a young woman in college, so that she might pray with it. She came to me for assistance after doing months of pastoral work in a very poor and medically impoverished part of Africa. She was emotionally depleted and near despair. Today, I would say she was traumatized by what she experienced there. Given her relationship with Love to that point, Linda did not expect the suffering she witnessed there to be overwhelming. It was. She also did not expect to feel so inadequate in her response to the suffering. She did. Love wasn't supposed to have such limitations. She had never had to face her own.

Linda then came back to a very demanding college program and a new, positive, but also very intense, romantic relationship that she wasn't sure she could trust. How could she trust love after what had happened to her? How could she trust her own love, let alone someone else's? Given her diminished and strained emotional resources, it was difficult for her to function—not just to study, but even to get out of bed each morning. She had major depression.

Since she was spiritually oriented, I tentatively suggested she use this story in her prayer. She could place herself in the story as a follower of Jesus, a follower who was overwhelmed by the suffering she witnessed on the sea and by the feeling that she was drowning. Or she could use the transformed story as a guide to tell Love directly her own recent story of following Love to Africa and being overwhelmed in the storm and by the limitations she experienced there, so much so that even back in the States she continued to feel she was drowning.

I said that whatever setting she chose, she should try to see Jesus or Love looking at her with compassion and inviting her to tell her story, her whole story, with its many continuing feelings. Prayer is a relationship, so I encouraged her to use this story every day, as long as it felt resonant with her experience. I also said that if at any point she feared she would drown and Jesus was sleeping, she should wake him up, again and again if necessary. All of this would be relating more intimately through prayer.

YOUR OWN PRAYER

First, call to mind your own story of trying to do good, being loving, following Love, having limitations, and being overwhelmed and disappointed in the midst of storms. Maybe you are in a terrible storm as you read this. You might find that this transformed Gospel story holds the feelings of your situation accurately and you can use the story as a frame for presenting your feelings to Jesus. Alternatively, bring your own story with all your varied feelings directly to Love.

Imagine Love waiting for you, seeing you, compassionately welcoming you and all your storm-related feelings. If the storm persists, if you are afraid of drowning and you feel Love is sleeping, wake up Love, again and again if necessary.

The stories in this book are not wrapped up with a bow. In fact, most don't come to a conclusion. They continue. The storms portrayed in them often recur. Our limitations remain. Often the suffering continues or has long-term effects.

The key to prayer is experiencing over time that we are in an ongoing relationship with Love before, during, and after whatever storm or suffering comes our way. It is a relationship in which expressing and sharing our experience is crucial, even when our experience is that Love sleeps at critical moments, even when we are angry.

Our feelings and experiences are human and natural. How could we not share them in relationship? We have all experienced how our own love knows suffering and never intends suffering. We can be sure that Love knows suffering, does not intend it, and responds compassionately to suffering and its effects.

Over time we can continue to orient ourselves to the relationship we have with Love, attune ourselves to it, and deepen it so that it will feel like a strong loving presence, a still point, even as we, those we care about, and the boats we find ourselves in are tossed about in violent seas. No matter the outcome, the still and loving point with all its compassion remains.

I do not know all the ways the trauma of Linda's experiences in Africa remained in her and affected her future life and relationships.

I do know that she was gradually able to trust life again and reorient herself to Love and relationships.

She eventually married the man she met in college after she returned from Africa. She relearned to trust love, and he learned to be supportive of the effects of her ongoing painful memories. Both were very generous toward the other. I gladly attended their wedding in a church nearby before they moved out of the area. After the ceremony, as I congratulated her and she thanked me, we both acknowledged that there would be more storms that would threaten her, as they do us all. It was clear that she felt better prepared and resilient.

I was only briefly in Linda's life. My role was to help her re-engage life, trust, and love. I did that with suggestions and perspectives, and fundamentally through a reliable caring relationship. Clearly her maturing relationship with her future husband was also key, and hopefully it continued to gain strength and to strengthen them both throughout their lives together. As you continue to read this book, you might keep an eye out for just how often positive caring relationships could be partial answers to the prayers of people who are suffering and cry out for help. So much of prayer is about relationship, the crying out for help, and the responses.

IMAGINE AND PONDER

- Even as we cry out in our storms and it seems Love is asleep, we are loving ourselves and our fellow sufferers. Why else would we cry out?

So our love is present and actively caring.

Could that also be Love being present?

Love present, Love caring, even if not calming the storm, even if facing limitations?

CHAPTER 2

LONGING

(Zechariah and Elizabeth Conceive a Son)

The following transformed story could resonate with most people. Most of us at one time or another have experienced longing or desire that has lasted years and been emotionally quite painful. For many, there is no end to it. Usually, it is longing having to do with someone we love or could love: To have a spouse or child return from war or prison, to conceive a child, to be safe from hunger and violence or other dangers, to find a good relationship, to establish a safe home, to form a healthy marriage, to have a loved one or ourselves restored to health. In all these ways, we desire to be made whole, and we desire for our relationships to be made whole. While praying with longing and desire, we wait and work with hope and are vulnerable. We also feel tendencies to anger, to give up, to become cynical, to harshly judge ourselves or others, and to despair. Longing and desiring are challenging and with time wear us down. Especially over years, it is difficult to sustain ourselves and hope, let alone flourish, while longing.

ZECHARIAH AND ELIZABETH CONCEIVE A SON

(Luke 1:5-25, 36)

Zechariah, a priest, and Elizabeth, his wife, desired a child for many years. While God recognized them both as good people, they were not able to conceive a child and then were considered too old. The couple's "barrenness" was seen as a disgrace by them and others. Still, one day the angel Gabriel appeared to Zechariah and told him they would have a son. Zechariah doubted the angel and was made mute until the birth of his son.

THE TRANSFORMED STORY

(What led up to this event? What else is happening?)

When there is a happy positive ending like there is for Zechariah and Elizabeth in the traditional story, we often don't calculate the suffering over years that went before that ending, and for sure we don't think of the many couples in similar circumstances whose longing didn't end so positively. Use this transformed story as a stimulus or model to bring your own painful longing or desire with all your varied feelings to Love.

It is unlikely Zechariah and Elizabeth were the only couple in their area that was childless. Imagine other couples nearby who also naturally expected to have a baby soon after their marriages but didn't. Most people at the time, from early in their lives, pictured themselves as husbands and wives and parents. Each child would be a living symbol of the couple's love for each other, and a joint focus of their overflowing loving energy. Now imagine each childless couple feeling first disbelief and then increasing fear, even dread, as each month of hope crashes in disappointment. Then years pass. They continue to long for a child, the positive difference a child could make in their lives, the love they so desire to pass on.

In addition to their own heartache and loss, they are slowly isolated in their community. They feel less support, more alone, and even feel blamed for something they are not in control of. Their community acts as if they are cursed and as if the curse might spread like a communicable disease. After a while these couples find each other amidst their isolation. As they meet, they gradually begin to question the harsh judgments surrounding each other. They experience these other childless people as loveable and loving. How could they also not be loved by God? Picture Zechariah and Elizabeth as one couple in this group. They begin to affirm these feelings in one another as Zechariah, a priest, leads their prayer to a compassionate God. As the years go by, the empty space that a child was meant to fill remains barren and tender. The grieving continues through the various phases of life. Oh, how each phase would have been different if only. . . .

And now imagine the reactions within this group to Elizabeth's pregnancy. Of course, they all rejoice with her and Zechariah, but they are devastated once again. They ache with unrelenting longing. Some other couple is blessed with a child; they are not. Why, Love? Why not us? Why stir our wound at all? The now-mute priest, Zechariah, goes with them to pray together as they have so many times before. Once again, they freely express their feelings to God—and they know for sure now God is present and listens because of how Elizabeth is blessed. They cry, "Why not answer all prayers? Do you have favorites? Aren't all good people deserving? Actually, aren't all people deserving? You give children to bad as well as good people! Who deserves to be without a child? We are crying out to you, the way your people have always done. Longing. We have cried for generations for a savior. Save us from our longing to love more. Don't you want us to love more?" They picture God listening to them, to all their feelings, even their anger, with the love and compassion they have learned to share with each other. This is prayer.

A CONTEMPORARY TRANSFORMATION

Whether you are longing for safety, food, a good relationship, health, a child, a home, or anything else, use the structure of the transformed story of Zechariah and Elizabeth to bring your own desires again and again to Love. During my over forty years of practicing psychotherapy, I learned that most of us long for or desire something over years. To be without it painfully limits the flow of love in our lives. We don't feel whole. Whatever it is we are missing feels like it could only help us love more. Use the following story as another model to share with Love your own longing, whatever it is for, with all its related feelings and consequences.

I know Sarah and Abe through my psychotherapy practice. They dream of having their own biological children as fruit of their love. They dream of contributing to the world as good parents of good children. Early in their marriage, after Sarah did not become pregnant, they actively focus for a year on trying to become pregnant. As the months go by, their fears mount. Their childlessness continues and could last. Inwardly they each feel they are moving closer to the edge of intense disappointment. They fear continuous grief. What if that which feels most meaningful might not in fact be possible? What if life limits them in this most significant way? When Sarah hears other people talking about their children or grandchildren, she breaks into tears. She shares this with Abe, and how she is becoming afraid to go out into the world. Her pain scares him. He longs to help his beloved as well as be a father.

Neither Sarah nor Abe is particularly religious, yet in ways that are natural and relational I see what they begin to do as prayer. They naturally turn to their relationships. Tentatively and vulnerably, they gradually share their experience and fears with people they are in good relationship with, longtime friends, some members of their families, and a medical doctor. They experientially test whether the responses they receive are compassionate and trustable. Most of their people do respond compassionately, without judgment and without assuming easy answers. Love is active, and once again it is easy not to be able to differentiate love and Love.

Sarah and Abe also reach out for medical fertility treatment. Clearly, their reaching out is another vulnerable cry for help. They do it tentatively, not knowing how their longing will be treated, whether they will feel compassion from the nurses and doctors for their fears and pain, not knowing if the doctors will think they can be helped, and not knowing whether any treatment they participate in will lead to their desired child. In addition to all this initial uncertainty, Sarah and Abe's subsequent steps into fertility treatment increase their monthly cycle of expectations and hope as well as disappointment. Some of Sarah's treatments come with physical and very stressful and intense emotional side effects. And then there is this: Just as we imagined how God positively intervened in Zechariah and Elizabeth's suffering but not with their similarly longing friends, medical interventions work for some other couples but not for Sarah and Abe. Sarah and Abe wonder explicitly, what is it about them? Are they defective in some way? Are the others special, more deserving? The feelings of anger and temptations to blame each other increase. Their crying out to whatever they hold as God also becomes explicit: Why me? Why us? If there is a loving God, help us! Why not?

In the midst of this painful turmoil, they also reach out to me and we begin our professional relationship. I want to help with the increasing emotional stress they are immersed in as a couple, which could easily rend their love. I do not talk with them about Love or God or prayer. I don't even consider it. I don't need to. They are already crying out for help, to those they know love them, and for loving action from their professional caregivers. This is the most natural prayer. Amidst crying out to have a child, they also are crying out for loving responses. Their network of love grows as friends, family, other professionals, and I respond to them. We try to hold them in active loving relationships even as they face limitations and suffer. Even if they don't pray consciously, some of us pray consciously for them.

LOVE IS PRESENT, HOLDS, AND SUSTAINS

Sarah and Abe never did have their own biological child, and while the acute daily pain of that loss subsided, the grief is always nearby to be felt. In fact, every year or so, certain happenings reliably trigger in Sarah a flood of tears as if a great internal dam bursts. In the midst of acute suffering or in periods when we relive that suffering, it is difficult for any of us to be aware of and appreciate being loved, even when it is sustaining. And it is difficult to have the energy and awareness to return love or love anew. That is especially true when we don't feel whole and are longing to love someone that we don't have with us, say someone far away in a battle zone, or when we are longing to love in a way that is not available to us—for example, to save someone from illness.

However, this is what also is true about Sarah and Abe: Over years, they gradually become more consciously aware of and grateful for their ever-expanding network of loving relationships. They feel comforted by this love and held by these relationships. What is more important and remarkable is that they feel moved to contribute to this network by actively returning that love when others need help, and by responding to, even inviting, new people into their lives and their circle of compassion and love. They now are part of Love's response to others' prayers.

IMAGINE AND PONDER

- Perhaps we all are longing to belong. Perhaps Love, too, longs for more relationship with each of us, among us and our world? Is it possible that all belonging is Love's prayer, what Love cries out for, Love's vision for evolution?

CHAPTER 3

SAYING "NO" TO GOD

(The Annunciation)

With chronic or traumatic pain and fear, it is not unusual to have moments when, in our most conscientious discernment, we decide to go against the established or usual interpretation of God's will or law. We may even feel we don't have a choice.

I transform this Gospel story to make room for such experiences. While it is easy to imagine this transformed story in the midst of questions around pregnancy and new life, it could easily be relevant to questions associated with the inherent limitations of life in any phase, even as death approaches.

THE ANNUNCIATION (Luke 1:26-38)

The angel Gabriel was sent from God to a virgin named Mary in Nazareth. She was committed to marry Joseph. The angel said to Mary, "Hail! The Lord is with you." Mary was greatly troubled. The angel reassured her, "Do not be afraid. God favors you." Then he went on to say, "You will have a son, and shall name him Jesus. He will be great, called Son of the Most High, and his kingdom will have no end." Mary said, "How can this be since I'm a virgin." Gabriel explained, "The Holy Spirit will come upon you, and the power of the Most High will overshadow you. Therefore the child to be born will be called holy, the Son of God.... Nothing will be impossible for God." Mary said, "Behold, I am the handmaid of the Lord. May it be done according to your word."

THE TRANSFORMED STORY
(What led up to this event?)

The transformation of this story begins prior to the angel Gabriel approaching Mary about being favored by God and being chosen to bear a son through the Holy Spirit. Feel free to use it as a model or change it in ways to help bring your long-term pain and fear to Love.

Imagine with me that there were other women Gabriel approached prior to Mary. Some were young like her, and others were older, virgins and not. They all said, "No."

One of the others was Helen, the same age as Mary, a virgin as well, but who also had older and younger sisters and a mother who was overwhelmed with taking care of them. A few of her older sisters were married and had begun having children at her age (between fourteen and sixteen years old). Helen loved her older sisters and witnessed how their lives were transformed in ways that seemed disheartening. They had to adapt to motherhood, adjust to different families, spend time with fewer and different friends, and shoulder more responsibilities, more aloneness, more weighty situations out of their control. Helen was frightened not just of the angel, but of what the angel's plan was *for her* after giving birth to a son and naming him. It seemed there was a plan for the son, but what about the mother? She could feel, even impulsively in the moment, that it would actually be too much for her. She was not ready to bear a child, let alone raise it, let alone take on marriage, all within a different family. She cried out, "No," and she ran.

Gabriel also came to Julie. She was in her twenties, a good mother, with a number of children already. She couldn't believe God wouldn't know how difficult her life was, the lives of her children, and the life of her husband. She let that angel know what was what! Julie also said she would gladly speak directly to God about it all. She was angry at the presumption embedded in what the angel was telling her. It didn't even sound like she had a choice. And she had already been putting her life on the line for her love for God and the family she already had and loved. She also said "No" to Gabriel, but she stood her ground, shaking inside, while looking directly into the eyes of the angel. She sobbed deeply and long after the angel left her. She felt terrible saying no to God, also disoriented and lost in ways, but still angry and sure of herself. Mostly, she felt alone.

That night, outside the dwelling where she lived with her family, she began laying out to God what had happened that day and all her feelings that were still so raw and sore. More nightly heartfelt talks followed, and they slowly came to feel like a conversation, the pattern of a deep relationship.

Eventually, Helen was able to do the same thing, speak to God in this open and full way, more and more over time, but for Helen it was years before she could engage that relationship.

A CONTEMPORARY TRANSFORMATION

I use this transformed version of the Annunciation as a framework to pray about a sensitive area of discernment in my life. It may model for you how to bring to prayer the difficult decisions that you face that could be surrounded by fear or emotional pain.

I have tried to orient and attune my life to Love. From the beginning of my education, training, and career as a clinical psychologist and psychoanalyst, I have felt called by Love to work with people in psychotherapy. I could not imagine any career that would be more meaningful for me and in which I could feel and be more loving with people.

However, the education and training for that career took me far from home. One of the very few times I have sobbed with sadness came as an undergraduate when I was talking with a gifted campus minister, Joe McTaggart, CSC. Unexpectedly, I suddenly burst into tears when I put into words a dawning realization: My parents dreamed of and sacrificed for the education I was receiving, yet they hadn't realized their sacrifices would continue. The opportunities they gifted me would likely take me far from what they themselves knew, and far from them geographically as well.

When I began practicing my profession, I remained far from home. There have been wonderful gifts that have come with my wife Pam and me meeting the challenges of creating a shared life in New England these last forty-five years. In the last eight years, though, as my mother navigates her nineties, my being at a distance from her as her physical and emotional health declines has been a source of suffering, for her and for me. I have always loved her and I have no doubt she has felt that love and appreciated how I expressed it. I also have felt and appreciated how she has valued my career without really understanding it and valued my life in New England even though it kept me at a distance from her. That emotional calculus has changed in the last few years as her life on her own has become more limited and difficult. While from a distance I have become more involved in her care, her needs continue to increase. The questions I ask myself are painful. Should I be with my mother more? Move near her? Have her come and live with us or near us in New England?

So here is a window into my prayer. I bring this all to Love: My mother's life and needs and my own. What does Love want? Love, of course, wants me to be physically closer to my mother. In this way, so far, I have said no to Love.

Love ALSO wants me to be with the people I love here, and to remain here with the lives I participate in daily, contribute to, and that feed me. In this way, I say yes to Love every day. I also am involved with the daily care of my mother from a distance.

In my prayer I see my Love looking at my mother with love, feeling her need, and trying to hold and comfort her as she struggles. I also see my Love looking at me with love, feeling my conflict, knowing my love for my mother and others, knowing my own needs, and, yes, holding me closely too.

Love is always presenting us with choices. Like Helen and Julie, I have not chosen to love in an all-or-nothing way. I have chosen to love in a way that may be different than what others desired, different from what my mother desires, and maybe even different from what Love most desires.

Every day I share with Love the decisions I am making around how I love and disappoint and even hurt my mother. The balance is becoming much more excruciating as my mother continues to decline and asks me directly when I visit, crying, "Why do you go away? Why don't you stay here?" In my prayer I have learned that Love is not put off by our choices. Love doesn't need to be protected from our choices. Love continually desires to be with us, before, during, and after our choices, always loving us. Although to be completely honest, a "No" to an angel may be easier than a partial no to my mother, a being I owe so much.

This is a dynamic situation that is changing even as I write this. It is inevitable that my mother will die. At this point it is impossible to know the timeline or the landscape of that final journey, and how closely and intimately I will travel it with her. What I do have a sense of and hope for is that my Love will remain with us both as we continue the journey, and as I have to make more decisions about her life and mine.

It does not go without saying that as my mother's health-care proxy and health-care power of attorney, I may face a more poignant version of this conflict as she enters the process of dying. What will Love want? And how will I respond? My Love wants my mother to have a full life, beginning to end, and my Love does not want and has never wanted my mother to suffer. I am very clear that I do not want my mother to suffer. I hope and imagine that my Love will continue to be with us, my mother and me, lovingly as we get to those final decisions and steps.

While I will write about Jesus and his dying friend Lazarus at another point in this book, here I cannot help bringing to our shared awareness an image that often comes to me as I pray with my mother's and my suffering. Jesus did not rush to Lazarus's side when he knew Lazarus was dying. He did not cure Lazarus from a distance as he did with others. Jesus also did not say no to Love. He continued to love Lazarus, but he said no to being with Lazarus until after Lazarus died.

Similarly, I imagine that Love would have understood that the women I imagined who said no to the announcing angel were not actually saying no to Love or God. These loving women continued to love. They said no to a particular choice they had about how to live loving lives. I can easily imagine Love understanding and looking on them lovingly.

Our relationships with Love continue through it all.

WE AND OUR RESPONSES ARE NEVER REJECTED

After sharing your heart with Love, what next? Well, the stories in this chapter clearly lead to two conclusions that are true for all the stories of suffering and prayer in this book. Since prayer is relationship and the suffering portrayed here is persistent: 1. We are called to continually share our hearts with Love, day after day. 2. Love will continue to listen and compassionately be present even as we disagree with or say no to some aspect of what Love may desire. Love will be present to the Helens and Julies and Tims who love in the ways they feel able and not in other ways.

We often actively imagine receiving responses of rejection to our most difficult repetitive feelings. It therefore is easy to overlook the beginning awareness of a long-term relationship when we first process that someone is finally, actually listening to us—even after we said no to them in some way.

So, one of the first things to look for is that you are not being rejected or judged negatively by Love. You may get bored with what you are expressing, you may have some embarrassment or shame in repeating it, and you may feel it is not being responded to, but it is important to imagine and then see that you are not being rejected. It may be unclear what Love will do actively and positively in response over time, but firstly use your imagination positively and gradually feel that Love is empathically seeing and listening to you. Let yourself gradually process, and eventually feel, compassion and acceptance.

IMAGINE AND PONDER

- Our refusals or disagreements are part of the long-term relationships we have with Love. Even as we disagree with or say no to some aspect of what Love may desire, even as Love says no to something we may desire, Love will not reject us and will continue to listen and compassionately be present with us.

CHAPTER 4

THE ANXIETY, HEARTBREAK, AND DANGER OF HUMAN DISPLACEMENT

(The Flight into Egypt)

It is 2025. I have been using this transformed story more and more often in my daily prayer. I have come to see more clearly that empathy, whether through direct experience or more indirectly, say through reading the news, is foundational to healing our world and leading it to wholeness. The capacity for accurate empathy, developed through relational experience and education, is necessary in order to deepen prayer. Empathy is also a necessary political capacity. "All men are created equal" is a statement of empathy. It is not only a philosophical proposition or spiritual tenet. And, of course, empathy has political consequences.

As of June 2024, according to the World Bank, there were 122.6 million forcibly displaced persons worldwide, and that number has been increasing each year. Many more people leave their homes before they are forced out and they do so under great psychological distress and with legitimate fear of what they are escaping and of what lies ahead. This chapter will help us pray not only for those people who must leave their homes or their homelands but also for their families and friends who are left behind, many in neglectful and dangerous situations themselves. It is also meant to help us pray for the people who do Love's work—that is, the loving work of trying to keep safe, care for, welcome, and make room for those who are displaced. And it is for those who, throughout each day, are facing the existential anxiety of deciding for themselves, for their own protection, to become displaced, and for those others facing the deep anxiety that some people do not care about them and will any day aggressively force them to leave their homes or the latest place they have settled while looking for safety and greater life.

THE FLIGHT INTO EGYPT
(Matthew 2:13–15)

In a dream, Joseph was told by an angel, "Rise, take the child and his mother, flee to Egypt, and stay there until I tell you. Herod is going to search for the child to destroy him." Joseph and his family fled that night toward Egypt. They stayed in Egypt until King Herod died.

TRANSFORMING THE STORY

To pray for those who are or could be displaced, even if it is you or your own family, let the transformed story help bring all the vulnerabilities in the situation to your heart and to your mind's eye. No matter how you have become familiar with displacement, whether it is through personal experience or through the news media, your empathy is a way to begin to see the way Love sees. Your empathy may be Love's call for you to respond to people who need your witness, your voice, your companionship. Those capacities can be powerful.

Try to see that Love knows and cares about each person who is vulnerable, knows how they are vulnerable, and is calling to them with love. Often this is shown through others' empathy. Love is a companion during the need to begin the journey and through each step, each day, each place of security, each situation of danger or damage, and while meeting each person along the way, friend and foe.

Whenever in the story you are moved to call or cry out to Love, or to respond to Love's call to you, do so. If it is every step of the way, so be it. Let Love know what you are feeling, no matter what the feelings are, and try to see Love respond with compassion. Try to let yourself be open to Love's compassion—both for you and for those for whom you are praying.

THE TRANSFORMED STORY

(What happens next?)

There are so many points of vulnerability when one has to leave home suddenly due to danger, especially after being awakened in the middle of the night. Any of these points could be the focus of prayer. For starters, would you trust and base a decision to upend your life on an anxiety dream? Would you trust a dream angel? Joseph and then Mary must have felt in their bodies that they were being called by Love, and that it was a dangerous calling.

Imagine the emotional pressure that Joseph and Mary were under to make crucial decisions in their frightened hurry to escape. What to bring with them? What to leave? Would their crying infant bring unwanted attention? What could be used to track them to Egypt? And who could be used? To wake others and say anything about what they were doing would put them at more risk. Even if they meant only to send messages back to friends and family in Nazareth who otherwise would not know what happened to them, wouldn't even that increase their risks? And did they know there was danger for other families, not only for themselves? Could they risk waking and warning others?

And what of their infant, Jesus? Being loved will help a child's resilience over time, but it doesn't protect children from being immersed in the fear of their parents or from the actual dangers in the situation. Anxiety is infectious. Danger doesn't respect age. The effects of trauma can be transmitted across generations.

There also is the vulnerability that they face on the journey itself. They already traveled by foot to Bethlehem with Mary pregnant. How could they make it to Egypt with a newborn? What monetary resources did they have left to travel? What official papers were they missing? Would news of King Herod's slaughter of young male infants travel faster than they could travel? When and how would they learn what had happened to the other families that they left behind in Bethlehem? How safe were the roads to Egypt? What routes would they take, and to where in Egypt were they headed anyway? Unfortunately, neither angels nor dreams are known for giving a lot of useful details.

They had to begin. They had to go quickly. Who else could they trust besides themselves? Who else could they try to care for? Their friends back in Nazareth? Other young families they had recently met around Bethlehem? Haste, fear, and desperation can narrow concern for others.

It is hard to know how to trust Love with one's own family, let alone others. Maybe they did tell one or two other families, ones they had recently met, and maybe one other family was able and willing to go with them. Then what? Was Egypt welcoming immigrants? Would it take in asylum seekers or deport them? And if they did make it into Egypt, how would they support themselves, where would they even begin to try?

Once established, how could they leave again? Even with Herod dead, would they be safe upon returning? Could they take that risk? Would they actually be welcomed back to their hometown of Nazareth given the violent aftermath of their leaving Bethlehem? Wouldn't there be social consequences for escaping? Would their neighbors trust them and feel they could be relied on? Can anyone really feel at home again, let alone safe, after being away for years and desperately adapting to a vastly different culture?

Then there is this: Can you ever feel safe after the world shows itself as so dangerous that you have to leave your home?

Can you feel the uncertainty Joseph and Mary felt? All the unknowns? The danger? The dream angel got them started toward Egypt. They must have felt Love with them, but they also must have felt so much vulnerability. They must have had doubts even as they hurriedly packed their belongings and prepared their infant son for travel. And if not doubts then, or the next day, or the day after that, then fears, the next day and the day after that.

They must have felt alone as they traveled. Except for their love. And even their love must have felt and been vulnerable.

See Mary and Joseph share their feelings about all their vulnerabilities with each other, within their love, and with Love, each day, multiple times a day. Using your own empathy as a guide, try to be open to and feel the compassion with which Love responds. Share your own feelings with Love regarding your own or others' vulnerabilities about being displaced. Try to see and feel Love's care for you and those others for whom you are praying.

CONTEMPORARY TRANSFORMATIONS

In recent years, with worldwide trends showing increasing and ever-widening disparities between rich and poor, the growth of autocracy vs democracy, billionaires overly influencing so many governments, isolationism, Christian Nationalism, and other exclusive religious movements, I have often remembered the story of an older Jewish friend and consultant. David grew up in the Netherlands just before WWII. One night while he was still a young teenager, his parents decided he needed to flee the coming occupation of the Nazis. They thought he had the courage and skills to make a good escape, and they thought he would be safer traveling alone. With only hours of preparation, he left that night and began a mostly nocturnal, dangerous journey across Europe. Eventually he was admitted into the United States even though other Jews were not. He finished his education, joined a profession, established a family, and became a beloved contributor to our society.

I learned this positive, straightforward story of David's early years only after many years of knowing him. There are parallels with the simple positive story in the Gospel of Jesus's young life. They both escaped a slaughter through emigration and eventually established a remarkable life. While positive endings may hide the suffering along the way so that outsiders may not see it, such endings do not make that suffering inconsequential.

I learned from David's wife that he did suffer along the way. He did not know what was happening to his family that he left behind. He felt anxiety and guilt. He was close to starvation on his journey. And there were many other painful details that he could not even risk letting himself remember post-trauma until he was an older adult. David described himself as an atheist, but in addition to remembering his despair, he also remembered moments of deep gratefulness and love. He told me about the woman he remembered (someone he tried to find later in life) who placed a couple raw potatoes outside the door of her tiny house in the woods each night. He found them, stole them, ate them in the woods, and had no doubt they saved his life. He knew they could have been the bait in a trap. He was desperate and still able to hope, trust, and be grateful. He was fed for three nights that way. He would be one of the first to say that love doesn't just show up at the end of a positive journey. It is with us all along the way, even when there are setbacks, when we despair, and even when the journey's end is terrible. When I pray for displaced people, I am thankful for David and how Love was with him. I am thankful for how his family and others loved him, and I pray with sorrow for how they all also suffered. David's whole story gave me a sense of how emigrants suffer and how they desperately need loving responses.

Another, more personal, contemporary, and ongoing story is that of a good friend, Luis, who left his home country in South America and walked across other countries, including Mexico, to get to our southern border. From praying with the transformed stories of Joseph and his family walking to Egypt and of David and his walking across Europe, I have an idea of what Luis suffered along the way—not the specifics, but the daily anxiety, the unknowns, the surrounding dangers, and the physical challenges. Like Joseph and his family and David, Luis crossed borders without papers. As a teen he walked into a city to find help and work as David and Joseph before him must have done. Luis, however, was detained in our country and placed in a prison for months. He was then deported back to his home country.

A year or so later, still not twenty-one years old, he tried again. I can't even imagine the desperateness, determination, and hope that would drive someone to take on the risks as well as the physical and emotional challenges of emigrating across multiple countries a second time, especially having already experienced that the odds were against him. When he reached our southern border the second time, he somehow trusted and paid a stranger to take him across the border in the back of a closed box truck. Many other displaced people were with him in that truck. That time, he was dropped off further from the border, and he then made his own way farther into the US.

Since entering the US over twenty years ago, he has begun his own successful business, paid taxes, established a family, and become a positive strong thread in the fabric of his community. He and his family have no criminal records. Like David's story, Luis's could be seen as a success for him and our country. That is, up until people in our country and government determined that they could win elections by playing on human fears and scapegoating immigrants, demonizing them. I only recently learned of Luis's story, years after I met him. What led to him sharing it was Pam and I inviting him and his young family on an outdoor educational day trip, a holiday excursion. They were too terrified to accept, terrified that they would be detained by US Immigration Customs Enforcement (ICE) agents.

As I write this, our government maintains that at any moment Luis could be legally detained by plainclothes, unidentifiable ICE agents with masks on, moved, briefly held anywhere in this country, and then without due process deported to any country our government might choose. If this were to happen with no one around, then his friends, my friends who know him, and Pam and I and his family might not even know where he is for days or longer, let alone be able to try to protect him and keep his vulnerable family intact.

In my prayer, remembering David and Joseph and his family's own vulnerabilities and displacement, I picture Luis companioned with Love every minute of every day in the midst of immoral if not illegal nationwide circumstances. Luis is a nontraditional spiritually oriented person, a loving person, a hardworking person, with a seemingly undefeatable positive and hopeful spirit that is contagious. One day, feeling helpless and afraid for him as I was praying for him and his family, it came to me that Pam and I could at least find and fund an immigration lawyer who would be available if he were detained. Given his circumstances, this effort might not protect him as much as anyone would want, but exercising our religious freedom might make what could happen more humane, move more slowly, and allow him and his family more knowledge, communication, and support. I am grateful for the ability to do something materially useful for Luis and for Love companioning us all.

Finally, there is Danny and his young family in Israel. They are friends from when they were working in the US for a few years. Even before the October 7, 2023, attack by Hamas, they were fearful about what was happening in their country. In addition to the ongoing threat of war, there were also political movements similar to those occurring in the US. Leaders were indicted for serious crimes, there were strong movements toward autocracy and the undermining of democracy, and there were extreme exclusionary religious positions. Danny and his family talked of emigrating to another country, but coming to the US again gave them pause given the very concerning changes in our own government. They were also reluctant to disrupt their children's lives and leave their elderly parents who did not want to leave despite the dangers. Then October 7th happened and everything worsened. The situation in Israel has not become more secure for families like Danny's. As I write this, Israel may be in the beginning stages of war with Iran. Danny and his family are frightened to stay in Israel, and they are frightened to leave. And there is always the chance that soon they will not have a choice.

As I fear and pray for Luis's family, I also fear and pray for Danny's. I pray Love continues to companion them in ways they can feel and that are useful. I realize I am part of the answer to those prayers, and I pray to attune myself to Love to ever more affectively support my friends as well as others as they face displacement.

INTERCESSORY PRAYER AND POWER

As you may have already noticed, I do not make unbounded claims for prayer or the Ultimate Loving Mystery we refer to as God. In fact, the whole point of this book is to help us acknowledge and face our common human experiences when we feel Love is not present or active in our lives. And yet...

And yet, I pray. In fact, I am writing to you about prayer, and this chapter alludes at a number of points to intercessory prayer, prayer asking for help. In my experience, the power of prayer, and what I have learned to ask for when I ask for help, is the attunement of myself and others to Love. I pray for myself and others to feel love, to be aware of love, to actively love, and to be grateful for love. Another way to say this is that I pray for myself and others to feel Love, to be aware of Love, to act with Love, and to be grateful for Love. All of that is what I mean by attunement to Love. It is attunement not in the sense of harmony but in the sense of empathy and accompaniment. There is power in loving accompaniment. There is power with Love.

IMAGINE AND PONDER

- Can you feel how your empathy can be Love calling to you to become aware and respond?
- Have you ever stopped in a day, a good day or a bad day, and tried to become aware of love in your life and the world? Or the effects of love in your life and the world? You might try to do so, even in this moment. Become aware and grateful.

CHAPTER 5

THE FAMILIES OF THE HOLY INNOCENTS

(The Massacre of the Infants)

This transformed Gospel story has particular value when we are facing truly innocent suffering, especially at a group or community level. When we or those we know, or even those we hear about, are the victims of some dreaded disease or natural disaster, this transformed story is a way to frame prayer. Alternatively, the situation could be a crime—a mass assault or killing of some kind such as a terrorist attack, school massacre, or war. It could address those innocently suffering some other injustice, from bullying and discrimination to unjust imprisonment.

Our prayer could address any or all aspects of this situation. Firstly, if we or our loved ones are suffering innocently, we can express that experience and all of our feelings directly to Love. Secondly, with Love we might share what's known as survivor guilt, a very common human feeling. For example, why were we spared while these innocents and their communities were devastated? Thirdly, as witnesses, we don't want the innocence or the suffering to go unnoticed, be forgotten, or not be grieved. With Love listening, we can share empathically in the pain, grief, and sorrow of the victims and their families.

Fourthly, we are morally confronted with the innocence of the suffering. Are we complicit? Have we done enough to help? With Love listening, we can face our responsibilities for others and we can face our guilt. Even in the original Gospel story, Love is implicated in the injustice. What else was happening as Jesus was born and began his life? Innocent boys were being slaughtered because of him. Love would understand any responsibility or guilt we feel.

THE MASSACRE OF THE INFANTS

(Matthew 2:16-18; associated with Jeremiah 31:15)

King Herod raged when he realized the magi had tricked him. He ordered the massacre of all the boys two years old and under in and near Bethlehem. The prophet Jeremiah's words were fulfilled: "A voice was heard in Ramah, sobbing and lamentation; Rachel weeping for her children; and she would not be consoled, since they were no more."

TRANSFORMING THE STORY

Recollect your own experiences of innocent suffering—something that you suffered or something that those you love or those you have heard about suffered. You can place yourself in the following story and let your experience be represented by the experiences of the families portrayed here. Alternatively, you could hold your experience close, and after witnessing how these families relate their suffering to Jesus or his mother, then you could do the same with yours.

THE TRANSFORMED STORY
(What happens later?)

You are in Jesus's time. It is around thirty years after the slaughter of the Holy Innocents. Everyone knows the story. Many from your village were there, around Bethlehem, and suffered through the horrifying reality. Some of your friends, perhaps even you, witnessed the slaughter of infant sons or brothers or nephews.

You are part of a group of families who have heard about the teacher and healer, Jesus. He has been doing such good in the surrounding areas. He is about to pass near your small village. Together, you are going out to hear and meet him. It is not lost on anyone who experienced that past time that Jesus is a man around thirty years old, was born in Bethlehem . . . and survived.

Imagine the time of day, the light, the landscape. Feel the heat or coolness of the day, the swells and bumps and ruts of the road as you walk. Notice the air and the smells it brings from the fields and hills. Hear the conversation of your friends, the anticipation of the coming meeting, and the mix of memories and feelings they stir—loss, anger, sorrow, curiosity, maybe wonder. You want to hear and experience Jesus the teacher, the healer, but his presence stirs other horrible memories and feelings as well.

Your group has reached Jesus. You see that he has already stopped with a crowd forming around him. You go closer and see him healing and preaching love. You notice that he actively welcomes little children to be with him even as he ministers and teaches. While he has never met anyone from your group before today, he notices you and your group as you arrive to listen and observe him. He welcomes you with his eyes and gestures to come closer. His eyes suggest recognition, sorrow, and perhaps some anticipation.

You might also see his mother, Mary, nearby, sitting alone. She is listening to him, but she also sees your group approach. She looks pleased that you have all come. In her, too, there seems to be recognition and sorrow, a touch of anticipation.

Whenever you are ready, approach Jesus or his mother and let them know who you are—a neighbor, brother, sister, father, mother of one of the Holy Innocents who died instead of him, you might even say died for him, so he might live. Let them know how you suffered and continue to suffer innocently, without having a choice. Express all the feelings you want them to appreciate and understand.

If it is the case that you have the very human feeling of guilt that you survived when others perished, let them know that feeling too. It would not be surprising if they also had similar human feelings.

If your own personal experience of suffering in your real life cannot be contained while you are imagining these families telling their stories, do not hesitate to also tell Jesus or his mother your own personal story of innocent suffering while they are here in front of you. Express your feelings as fully as you can to make sure they appreciate and understand what you witnessed or experienced, what you felt and feel.

Jesus is present. He is listening. His mother is present and listening. You are engaged with Love. This is prayer.

See Jesus and Mary hear and understand you. They are compassionate in the face of whatever feelings are in you—suffering and loss, even your anger, rage, and accusations. Notice they are not strangers to suffering. Neither are they strangers to anger or judgment. They are not put off by it.

Know also that both Jesus and Mary feel they were indeed fortunate to survive the slaughter. Know that each is painfully aware of your sacrifice for them.

Jesus listens. How does he look as you talk to him and share your experiences? How else does he respond? How does he move? What does he do?

Mary listens. How does she respond in her face, her body, and her actions?

They may have something to say to you directly. More likely, you feel they will gladly sit quietly with you, sharing your feelings, for as long as you desire.

A CONTEMPORARY TRANSFORMATION

I wrote the first draft of this chapter just days before the killings of twenty young children and their six teachers and administrators at Sandy Hook Elementary School in Newtown, Connecticut, on December 14, 2012. I first prayed with this transformed story with all those innocents held in my mind and heart. There have been many similar, terrible mass killings since then that also evoke this story and prayer. There have been long and devastating wars. There have been killings of innocent black men and women by police that, while not mass shootings, have added up each year to more sickening numbers. There are many innocent immigrants at our borders. There is bullying in our schools and on social media, and there are many innocents in our prisons. All of these humans have families and friends who suffer with them, and who continue to care deeply for them. And this happens all around the world every day.

Darrell Jones was in prison while innocent for thirty-two years in Massachusetts. He was sentenced at eighteen years old to death-in-prison, or "life," for a murder he did not commit. It is estimated that 1 to 5 percent of the 2+ million people in US prisons are innocent, somewhere between twenty and one hundred thousand of our fellow citizens.

When I pray about innocent suffering, I imagine Love waiting for me, wanting to hear my experience, and already knowing and holding the whole picture. As a witness, I share my feelings about the injustice of innocents suffering. I share my horror at, and empathy for, their pain.

In Darrell's case, I share my feelings about the basic details I know of how overwhelmingly difficult it was for him to adjust to prison at eighteen years old—the lack of freedom, lack of support, aloneness, and the dangers—all the while innocent. I wince and share my empathic ache as I think of how he grew up while in prison—grew up for thirty-two years of his life into an older adult. If you were fortunate to go away to college at eighteen, imagine going to prison instead. Imagine being mostly confined, not to a dorm room, but to a cell until you're fifty years old.

As part of my witnessing, I picture how what-might-have-been was lost for this smart, articulate, positively motivated, always active man. And I grieve. Add the losses that assailed him while he was alone and imprisoned alone—the death of a son, the death of a brother, and the death of his beloved grandmother. And I know only a small fraction of his story.

I came quite late into his story. He sought "an outside" therapist, eventually me, while he was still in prison because he did not want "to turn into a hating animal." I give thanks in my prayer that his capacity for love not only survived but increased and found expressions in prison even in the midst of so many forces trying to dehumanize him. I am thankful that Love was somehow with him in prison in ways he sometimes could feel, even though at other times he could not help but despair.

As I pray, I picture Love listening with empathy, even to my very human sense of survivor guilt. There were numerous times in court when I listened to the events that led to his imprisonment. I often felt how fortunate most of us are not to be in the wrong place at the wrong time. Love is familiar with this kind of suffering.

There is more to my prayer than witnessing and survivor guilt. While King Herod in the original Gospel story may have been an extreme individual, his desire for safety, protecting his position and life, should not be unrecognizable in ourselves as we want to feel protected from danger and losing our own privileged positions in society.

Darrell was most probably framed by unjust elements in our justice system. His trials were *The Commonwealth of Massachusetts v. Darrell Jones*. They were not *The Corrupt Members of the Brockton, MA, Justice System v. Darrell Jones*. The Commonwealth of Massachusetts is my fellow citizens and I. We want protection and do not see, do not want to see, what injustices are often done in our names with our implicit disavowal of responsibility.

When I pray for any of the world's suffering innocents, their families and friends, and for those like Jesus and his mother who can feel guilty for surviving, I also pray for the parts of me that want protection and do not see, do not want to see, what the unjust elements of our system of justice do with our disavowal of responsibility, our role in reinforcing others to do evil in our names—all through our silence.

As I pray, I imagine Love is listening with empathy.

Exonerated and free now, Darrell Jones is a good friend, but there is not a time when I think of him that I do not also think of how I am not doing enough to stop actually lived stories like his unfolding even as I write this. Of course, I pray for other innocents, hold them in my heart and mind, but I also pray to understand my own mixture of innocence and responsibility for what is done while I am inactive and silent. I pray to find ways to act for justice, and my actions for justice are prayer too.

I express sorrow for the suffering that remains from Darrell's terrible experiences during those thirty-two years. I am thankful he survived, that his love survived, and, despite his continuing suffering, that he works every day to help other innocents obtain justice. I give thanks to Love for Darrell's and my friendship. I am thankful for the fact that I know him. My life and love have been enlarged for knowing him. I am thankful to have met his family and friends. I feel privileged to have been a support during his last years in the high-security prison, his appeals, and his eventual retrial, all those struggles with and challenges of our system of justice.

I question Love too. How could Jesus face the Innocents' families? How could he live with his care and sorrow for them, knowing his role in their pain and suffering?

Love holds all of this, and more. Love holds Darrell. Love holds me as I share it all, and Love wants to hear it all, even over and over, after every time I talk with Darrell, and sometimes even just when I think of him.

All this is what my own personal prayer looks like as I pray for Darrell and how his life, suffering, and love affects my life.

PRAYER AND MORE RELATIONSHIP

Innocent suffering, especially on a mass level, is often both horrifying and unimaginable. It is easy to feel powerless and overwhelmed, easy to fairly quickly move on to thinking about something else.

You might try to imagine, see, sense Love waiting for us to face and share what innocent suffering stirs in us. Love is waiting for us to engage Love's presence in relationship by sharing the natural feelings that come with our very human attachment to all our brothers and sisters in the world.

Try to imagine, see, sense how Love is familiar with suffering. Love wants to companion us, to be in relationship with us, in our suffering and in our responses. It doesn't matter whether our feelings come with tears or loud rants, whether they overwhelm us, whether they include anger, fear, sorrow, guilt, or the shocks of how little control we have and what harm we humans can do to each other.

Most fundamentally, what is important to imagine and then look for is a sense that Love wants relationship. Our expressions of feeling open the door for relationship and the healing that comes with being connected to Love in our lives through loving. What might this look like?

Well, as I was competing this chapter, a new thought came to me. What if the answer to my praying for the families of Newtown, Connecticut, in 2012 was my later relationship with Darrell Jones? After all, Love works through loving relationships. We'll never know for sure. That's the nature of truth being a relationship and not a belief. However, it makes me wonder and be a little wary regarding what's in store for me after all the praying with Love I have done for Darrell. Who else will be coming my way or is already waiting nearby as a way for Love to call me and a way for me to answer? I am looking for more relationship.

IMAGINE AND PONDER

- Love is familiar with suffering. Love is waiting for us to share what suffering stirs in us.
- Our expressions of feeling open the door for more relationship. Love wants relationship. Who is coming my way, or is already waiting nearby, as a way for Love to call me and a way for me to answer Love's call?

CHAPTER 6

THE OVERWHELMED YOUNG ADULT, AGE THIRTEEN TO THIRTY

(The Hidden Life of Jesus)

This period of Jesus's hidden life (between age thirteen and age thirty) is rich with possibilities for praying with suffering. If there is some specific source of pain that you cannot find a narrative frame for in the Gospels or other scripture, you might try to imagine Jesus facing it during this time of his life, either in himself or others.

THE BOY JESUS IN THE TEMPLE (Luke 2:41–52)

After his parents found Jesus in the Temple, "sitting in the midst of the teachers, listening to them and asking them questions," he returned to Nazareth with them. Then begin eighteen years that are commonly called "the hidden years" of Jesus. They are hidden because there are no references to him in the Gospels during that time of his life. This is the sentence that begins that period of his life: "And Jesus advanced [in] wisdom and age and favor before God and man." The Gospels next pick up the story of his life when he is around thirty years old and comes back into public view.

A CONTEMPORARY TRANSFORMATION

Marta, a young woman in her twenties with whom I worked for a few years, wrote me when I was already retired and finishing the first draft of this book. She shared with me her hopes and significant efforts at trying to get established in life—to have a job, a career, a place to live, friends, and a romantic relationship. Due to her efforts, you could say she was gaining experience and "advancing in wisdom." Nevertheless, mostly, her efforts failed. She was learning how very difficult it is for single young people to find jobs and relationships that are substantial enough to build a life with, without continual anxiety.

In a follow-up phone conversation, I told Marta to imagine that Jesus had similar experiences to hers, that he couldn't find ways at first to make a living, find a place to live, and find affirming friends that would help him get established. It is not a sin to try and fail, but maybe failure is why we don't know more about those hidden years.

Especially in occupied lands and countries where there is extreme inequality in the distribution of wealth, it is problematic for young people to successfully get established. It is easy to see how the young adult Jesus, having trouble getting launched in life, could be tempted to give up hope and how he could have empathy for his friends who did give up or picked extreme alternatives—for example, becoming a violent revolutionary. One could imagine his anger at the structures of his society that oppressed his and his friends' flourishing. Similar economic structures undermined Marta's efforts even though she was very talented and caring. She was only hired without benefits to very low-paying part-time jobs that didn't need her level of education. Her supervisors were undermining, and the pools of potential friends she was introduced to often overflowed with self-centered people who wanted only to be around successful and beautiful people who made them look good.

Marta wrote to me after we stopped working together because she hoped I would still be interested in her challenges. I was. I suggested she imagine Jesus waiting to hear of her challenges, even calling to her. I suggested she respond to him. Just as she did with me, she could share with Jesus her own and her friends' experiences and feelings about trying to get their lives well grounded.

Marta had already established a prayer relationship with Jesus when she was in college. I was hoping my suggestions would help bring more of her current continuing suffering into her relationship with Jesus. I hoped their relationship would deepen with this sharing.

Those of us who address God as Love or in some other way can use an imaginative story about Jesus as a way of framing and illustrating how we are suffering, and then we can bring that experience and the related feelings directly into our prayer.

THE ROLE OF IMAGINATION IN PRAYER

No other chapter is as spacious as this one in its openness to imaginative possibilities regarding Jesus's early life. There is great freedom and there are many possibilities to imagine our own suffering within a personally transformed story that actively involves Jesus between the ages of thirteen and thirty. Just as I tried to do with Marta, I want to strengthen your ability to feel that invitation.

The image I am about to share with you came to me years ago after my first meeting with my spiritual director, Bill Barry, SJ. It comes out of the long Christian mystical tradition of praying imaginatively that was greatly developed by Ignatius of Loyola (1491–1556).

This image radically changed my worldview forever. It also fundamentally affirmed the way I pray with suffering. Here is the image: *I see Love continually gazing at each of us with compassion and joy, calling us, and patiently hoping we will respond consciously.* Within everything we experience, whether it be a sunset, a newborn kitten, an eagle in flight, a wonderful friendship, or chronic suffering, Love is *already* compassionately present and lovingly looking at us, calling us to share our experience. We don't have to prove ourselves through action or belief. Love has already judged us to be loveable. While we may have to become aware and open our eyes, we don't have to search and call out—though it is very human to do so. Love is *already* present, with us, close, and reaching out to us—first. Love wants to know us more, both through our own words and how we respond without words. All of the transformed stories in this book are grounded in this worldview, grounded in Love loving us *already* and continually.

That image of Love looking at us with joy and compassion, and waiting for our response, is respectful of our individuality and also spacious, totally open to any and all possibilities we feel, think, or imagine. Love wants to know us and, I believe, wouldn't mind being surprised. If there ever was a time or place to feel free and creative and honest, this would be it, in the light of Love's gaze. With this image, I am more vulnerable in my prayer, more honest, more intimate; I trust Love more to be able to accept and understand my feelings, including my anger; I am more confident and joyful that I am loved; and I feel Love appreciates my engaging in relationship, my trying to know and attune myself with Love and Love's creative action in the world. I hope you will test out this image and world-view for yourself.

IMAGINE AND PONDER

- Imagine Love always and everywhere, *already*, *now*, seeing you within the whole of all your experiences and feelings, including all your suffering. Imagine Love's eyes, *already*, *now*, looking at you with compassion and joy. Imagine a response rising within you, and Love patiently waiting for that response.

CHAPTER 7

THE SUFFERING FAMILY

(The Parable of the Prodigal Son)

This transformed story delves into how complicated and long-lasting the connections and consequences are among people who are suffering. The focus here is on a family. When one person in a family is identified as very problematic, typically each member of the family suffers in some significant way.

The problem could be addiction, psychological illness, or continual conflict or rebellion. Not only is each individual member affected but also the communication and love among them can become more strained. The entire family could easily turn cold, even hostile, and break apart. Sometimes sections of the local community are affected and become involved. Sometimes sides are taken and the conflict expands.

THE PARABLE OF THE PRODIGAL SON (Luke 15:11-32)

In this well-known story, the youngest of two sons comes to the father and asks for his inheritance. He leaves with it and squanders it all.

Over time he experiences dire need and acts in even more shameful ways. Eventually he decides to return to his father, express his sorrow over his hurtful behavior, and ask to be treated as a hired worker. As he returns, his father sees him a long way off, is filled with compassion, and runs to meet and embrace his son. The son expresses his sorrow, and in response the father welcomes him back as a true son. He orders a feast to celebrate, saying, "This son of mine was dead and came to life again; he was lost and has been found."

The older son is working in a field when his brother returns. When he hears the celebration and what it is for, he angrily refuses to participate. The father pleads, and the older son replies, "Look, all these years I served you and not once did I disobey your orders; yet you never feasted in my honor. But when your son who swallowed up your property with prostitutes returns home, for him you slaughter the fattened calf." His father says to him, "My son, you are here with me always; everything I have is yours. But now we must celebrate and rejoice because your brother was dead and has come to life again; he was lost and has been found."

TRANSFORMING THE STORY

A book could be written about all the ways this story could be transformed to reflect the challenges and suffering that a family goes through. The variations of suffering and the variations in the stories about that suffering are endless. In line with this fact, it is easy to imagine that Jesus told this same basic story—a family suffering with a problematic member—many times with many variations during his public life. For example, he could have told it about an alcoholic father leaving his spouse and young children.

In this telling, the father might return in sorrow and be forgiven by his family.

In the stories that follow, there are four family members. (In the Gospel story there are three. In the Gospel telling, the mother's or women's role in the story is missing. One could imagine that fact itself could be reflective of some suffering within the portrayed family and in the culture of the time.) You may be like any one of the four people in the stories of the families that follow. Alternatively, at any given moment you might find parts of yourself simultaneously identifying with each of them.

Described simply, the four possibilities are:

1. **A problematic member.** For example, a person who is addicted or counter-dependent/oppositional.
2. **A forgiving, responsible, and anxious point person in the family.** Usually this is a parent, or perhaps a "parentified" child.
3. **A responsible member of the family who also feels disrespected.** Often a competitive sibling.
4. **Another member feeling helpless while loving each of the others.** Perhaps the other parent, in the wings out of choice or relegated there.

All are suffering. There are also community members nearby, friends, who care about what happens to this family as a whole and to each member. Additionally, there are other members of society who want the disorder to go away and tend to stress the rules and limitations of the situation.

THE TRANSFORMED STORY
(What happens later?)

Use this story to help bring to prayer your own experience of suffering embedded in long-term relationships.

Imagine that you feel that you have been drawn here this day. You are sitting near Jesus as he teaches about the kingdom of heaven. The authorities are nearby grumbling that Jesus welcomes and eats with sinners. Picture him sharing with the crowd the painful story of a family like yours—his story of the prodigal son. At the conclusion, with a compassion you can feel, he surprises you by motioning for you to tell your similar story. He must know your story doesn't have a clean conclusion like his. In contrast, yours continues.

You nervously stand and self-consciously raise your head. You begin, as loudly as you can: "There is a daughter who leaves home. She is compelled to satisfy an addiction. At her most despairing, when the addiction has led her to shameful depths, perhaps after a hoped-for partner has abandoned her, she decides to go back home. She intends, shamefully, only to ask for a place to stay while she repairs her broken life. Her mother sees her coming, runs to embrace and kiss her, and welcomes her back with love that touches the heart of this strong-willed daughter and the hearts of everyone who witnesses this wondrous occurrence. Since the young woman left home, the community has been supportive of the mother and hopeful regarding her daughter's return.

"The daughter's older sister was also hopeful, but she is also jealous of the attention her sister is now getting. She is resentful about what feels like rewards for her sister's dangerous and hurtful behavior. She refuses to be a part of the homecoming celebration for her sister. Their mother seeks her out and explains to her older daughter, 'My dear daughter, you are always with me, and all that I have is yours. But we have to celebrate and rejoice, because this sister of yours was dead and has come to life; she was lost and has been found.'

"Over the next few days, both the mother and older sister notice that things about the house are missing, valuable things like pieces of jewelry, cash from the hidden savings box at the back of the highest shelf, and other things as well, like articles of clothing. They begin to fear that their beloved sister/daughter is still very troubled. They worry about a powerful addiction, an intense desire for some exciting partner to transform her life, and a compelling need to feel autonomous and powerful.

"One morning before daybreak, the day her mother and sister were planning to confront her, the troubled daughter secretly leaves again. More is missing from the house.

"Once again, she is not heard from for weeks. The father of the family is supportive of his wife and elder daughter. He feels compassion for his youngest. Mostly he is overwhelmed with grief. The community surrounding the family is again upset as they hear about what happened. Some members are angry at the daughter, some are sad with empathy knowing they all have tried hard to make their family whole, some offer to help, a few others who have been envious of the family are pleased, and there now are a few who angrily say, 'Good riddance.'

"A pattern of emotionally difficult leave-takings and emotional returns is established and continues. Again and again, the daughter returns home only to leave after days or weeks, and always everyone involved feels miserable. Each family member is more and more afraid about what will happen next, how this period of family life will end. Each is frustrated, even angry with the limitations each one faces."

You stop there. You haven't identified which person you are, but your weariness is now evident. To the crowd you appear older than when they first saw you stand to share your version of a family suffering. You sit again and are only aware of Jesus holding you with his eyes full of compassion. Not all, but most in the crowd feel similarly. You sense their support.

Your coming here, your responding to Jesus's invitation and sharing your story, this is the beginning of prayer and what will be a long relationship.

A CONTEMPORARY TRANSFORMATION

I knew a mother, Cynthia. She did not have an easy early life. However, she managed to have a high-powered, albeit brief, career and a marriage to a responsible man who also had a high-powered career. Both of their daughters had significant learning disabilities, were non-neurotypical, and had problematic anxieties. The parents loved their children. Even with that fundamental support, however, school was difficult for both children. They did not fit well with other students or their teachers. The daughters didn't meet their own expectations, let alone those of their parents. Both were intelligent, but they didn't feel like it or look it to others. They were both very unhappy.

Cynthia quit her career to help her daughters through their school years. She did not want them to feel as abandoned as she herself did growing up. She tried her best to support them through challenges and smooth their way interpersonally with others. She was just their loving mother though, not a fairy godmother, and definitely not God.

The elder of the two daughters, Diana, gradually turned against her mother. She blamed her mother for her not fitting in. She felt her mother wasn't helpful, but overbearing. She said many times that if only her mother had done things differently, she would fit in and be happy. As Diana went through high school and into college, she lost jobs, boyfriends, and roommates despite her mother's best advice and guidance. She always wanted money. Her unhappiness and anger increased. Eventually she moved across the country to live on her own, far from her mother's influence and daily loving efforts. Her mother and I wondered about the daughter's abuse of alcohol or other drugs/medications.

The younger daughter, Stephanie, had a more difficult time in school. However, somehow, she trusted throughout that her mother had her best interests at heart. She was frustrated by her limitations and others not understanding her, but she kept plugging away at the challenges she faced. In the midst of them, she knew her mother loved her and that she loved her mother. Diana was angry at how the younger daughter, her sister Stephanie, was "babied" by her mother. She said her sister needed to grow up and be less protected by their mother. She felt her mother was undermining Stephanie's independence.

Both girls admired their father, who often was not home because he was working to support the family. They did not criticize him and desired his positive attention. They would not speak with him about their difficulties or their anger. While supportive of his wife's responsibilities for their daughters, he did not get involved in their conflicts. Interpersonal conflicts were not his area of expertise. He was concerned about his elder daughter, but his focus tended to be on what his wife could do differently to make the situation better, to make for less hostility. Truth be told, he was a bit afraid of Diana.

At one point, Diana lost a job and was considering moving back to her hometown and into her younger sister's small, shared apartment.

As she was planning this, she continued to criticize her mother, her sister, and even her sister's suite-mate.

What was Cynthia to do?

Of course, she loved Diana and wanted to help her. She knew empathically that Diana was feeling humiliated that she even needed help, let alone needed to ask for it. Maybe Diana's assuming the family's support in this situation was a sign that she understood that she was loved by her family. Cynthia intuitively knew that if she in any way hesitated to help or blocked Diana's plans, Diana would be furious and it would be evidence to Diana that her mother never loved her. She felt guilty that she was ambivalent about giving Diana what she wanted.

Cynthia also wanted to protect Stephanie. For her part, Stephanie loved and wanted to visit with her sister, but she was terrified Diana might move in and stay, making her life miserable and perhaps ruining her relationship with her suite-mate, her first-ever very positive and stable friendship. Stephanie also felt guilty about her mixed feelings.

As for her husband, Cynthia wished he could understand why she was so anxious about the extreme consequences of any position she might take in regard to Diana moving in with Stephanie. On the one hand, he couldn't see the big deal in Diana's moving. He thought his wife was overreacting. On the other hand, he remembered the tension in their house when Diana lived there, and he wanted Cynthia to place strict rules and restrictions on her once she was with Stephanie. He wanted this even though restrictions and rules had never worked in the past with Diana. He could feel himself avoiding or staying away from the tension he felt in his wife and in their conversations. He had some feelings of guilt about this behavior, but he turned his focus back to work where he felt good about the authority and power he had to get others usefully in line and make positive things happen.

Then there was Diana and the intensity of her extreme feelings. She desperately wanted help, but she couldn't bear to ask for it, an act that in her eyes would be humiliating. So, she planned and expected to be able to do just what she wanted, as usual, in order not to be vulnerable, not to be rejected outright. She knew people were afraid of her and her anger, and that they had reason to be angry at her. However, her self-understanding didn't get her as far as taking responsibility for her actions or dealing with her own guilt.

THE BEGINNING OF PRAYER

Each person in these situations prays. Each father, each mother, every son, and every daughter, they all are suffering, and at least internally crying out with their pain—to the universe, to a friend, a family member, a mentor or wisdom figure, or to Jesus or Love. Love is already lovingly calling to and waiting to hear from each person. Our desire to cry out is a response.

I know Cynthia cried out explicitly to God, continually. I am certain she hoped for quick resolutions, but even when they weren't forthcoming, she felt she was in an ongoing relationship with God. That relationship did not just help her feel less alone in her challenges and frustrations. She also felt affirmed and aided in her continuing efforts to be attuned to love when she was talking with her husband, Diana, or Stephanie. Amidst these very difficult relationships, she was at least partially sustained by her relationship with God.

What makes suffering so difficult in families and other long-term relationships is that it often doesn't end. Maybe one can see gradual improvement over many years and much hard work. The problems seem to get better or even vanish for periods. However, the problems often continue or return, maybe at lower levels of intensity, and usually there is an ongoing vulnerability: When will things get worse again? How bad will they be?

In reading these stories, you are being invited to take time and become aware of your own continuing suffering that is touched by them. Try to see how Love is calling you—yes, even right now—how Love wants to know you more deeply, wants to hear in your own words about your experience. You are already in a natural relationship with Love. Prayer makes that relationship more explicit and more intimate, more of a conscious sharing. More reliable than the pain you may feel is the call for more relationship. It also isn't just here today and gone tomorrow. Love wants to hear from you day after day, even when you are repetitive in your crying out and wanting relief.

The context for our prayer is often imaginative. Picture Jesus in the Gospel having just told his story of the prodigal son. Then see him lovingly invite us to share our own personal, very specific stories. Imagine yourself in the crowd and sharing your story with Jesus, or imagine sharing it with him when you two are alone together. Picture how Jesus lovingly sees and hears you as you share.

Another way to begin praying is to put the Gospel versions aside. Begin by bringing Love to mind. This involves a less specific kind of imagination. Open your heart enough to directly express your story of suffering. Share what you know of each family member's suffering—father, son, mother, brother, sister, or even concerned friend or community member. Maybe the transformed versions you just read helped you to become more conscious of your suffering with your family, or more aware of how your other family members are fragile or suffering.

Responding with your own story to the compassionate interest of Jesus or Love is you beginning to intentionally pray and relate in a way that will deepen over time. Continue to express your feelings every day. Over time, try to look for and attune yourself to a loving response.

PRAYER AND RELATIONSHIPS

These stories of suffering families are in fact familiar. If they do not resonate with your own family's experience, it is likely you recognize the families of people you care about. When families suffer, they tend to want to keep that fact secret as if it is an embarrassing weakness. That is a sign of a fear of negative, humiliating judgment and painful feelings of being too alone.

One of the most important things to look for as we relate more to Love in our prayer is more and deeper relationships in our lives generally. A family suffering is actually quite difficult to keep secret. However, over time, as you express yourself to Love and are listened to with compassion, you may be drawn to others with whom you will want to risk sharing your story. You can see this as a partial answer to your prayer. You may feel strong enough to risk expressing yourself to them. You may be resilient enough to try with someone else even after your first effort goes unmet. This also is prayer—continuing, deepening. Some people, like Love, will listen compassionately and be affirming of your true self and your loving efforts. Some may even have been waiting for you to come to them. In a less intense way, you also could notice people unexpectedly smiling at you as you go through your day, being courteous toward you, or reaching out in some small or large way. It could be that you will meet new friendly people who will want to be with you in ways that are enjoyable that have nothing to do with your family—for example, someone who may like walking each morning like you do or gardening or shopping.

The major sign that your prayer is being heard and actively responded to is when prayer increases or deepens relationships. Relationships are life-giving and contribute to wholeness.

IMAGINE AND PONDER

- Relationships are often what we pray about, and often they can be partial answers to our prayer. When we share our suffering within our relationships, they embody our prayer.

CHAPTER 8

GUILT

(The Call of Matthew)

This transformed Gospel story is for those who suffer with guilt. It is also for those who are pained by regret, wishing the impossible, that they could do the past over again, differently. It is a story that helps one to acknowledge that sometimes guilt is deserved. It is a painful feeling that can last for years, even with forgiveness. And yet, there is always more to one's life.

This story is also for those who stand by and respect those who are guilty, who see that what the guilty persons did wrong is only a part of them, a part they have sorrow for, a part they can actively work to learn from and reform.

THE CALL OF MATTHEW

(Matthew 9:9-13; also see Mark 2:13-17 and Luke 5:27-32)

Jesus was passing through and saw a tax collector sitting at his post. Jesus said, "Follow me." The tax collector got up and followed Jesus. It was not unusual for tax collectors and sinners to eat with Jesus.

Pharisees asked why he ate with such people. Jesus responded with two sayings: "Those who are well do not need a physician, but the sick do" and "Learn the meaning of the words, 'I desire mercy and not sacrifice.'"

THE TRANSFORMED STORY
(What happens next?)

Imagine the Pharisees leave Jesus and his followers after his words about mercy. There are other people who remain, however, who are also upset with Jesus, particularly his welcoming of Matthew. They are Matthew's victims. They were overcharged by Matthew or shown no mercy by him when they couldn't pay their taxes on time. They and their families were taken advantage of. Crushed with debt. Impoverished.

There is silence as Jesus warmly looks directly at each of them, and they feel the urge to come close to where Jesus sits with Matthew. Jesus clearly is waiting for them to speak, encouraging them with his expression and eyes.

So, they do. They speak with hurt and anger regarding Matthew, and despair over their circumstances. Jesus continues to look at them with love, and his own sadness deepens as he listens.

This is the beginning of their prayer.

Matthew looks toward them too, knowing they speak the truth. His body seems to fold down and in with the weight of so much truth and the consequent guilt.

After they finish speaking, Jesus continues to be present to them. Silently. Only after a long silence does he turn to Matthew. Everyone can see both his sadness and care for Matthew. Matthew sees them too. Then Matthew begins to speak. Slowly. Honestly. With great feeling behind the words. Jesus is listening. Matthew tells his story, his feelings, his experience, honestly. This is the beginning of his prayer.

Most of the people who were hurt and damaged by him are listening too. They are open, wanting to know him, hoping they might understand something that would be useful in their terrible situations. Their seeing Jesus listening and their own listening to Matthew is their prayer continuing. They are beginning to get a response.

A CONTEMPORARY TRANSFORMATION

Matthew must have stressed and angered many people financially and emotionally. Taxes were not just burdensome. They funded an oppressive occupying force. They also were a means of social control, keeping people subservient, too needy to risk resistance.

In contrast to Matthew's job, mine as psychotherapist was all about helping relieve people's suffering or helping them to develop well and even flourish. Jesus called Matthew from a hurtful job. I always felt that my job was my major response to Love's call to me.

However, now retired after forty-two years of doing psychotherapy full-time, I've had a lot of time to review my work helping to relieve people's suffering. While I appreciate all the good that I contributed and am grateful for the opportunities to participate in people's growth, I have become acutely aware of the times I hurt or harmed people. When memories and feelings about my being hurtful return, I reframe those experiences into contemporary versions of Matthew's transformed story that I can use in prayer. What follows is an example.

Near the beginning of my career, Nate and I were working well together. He was a graduate student in a counseling program. He clearly felt that his consultations with me were helpful. I could see and feel his appreciation and growing trust of me. Then his father died. He let me know the upsetting news through a message. We did not meet for a few weeks.

When we eventually met next, I was expecting us to talk about his feelings for his father, his loss, and how he managed his difficult family during this crisis. While we did speak briefly about those, I could feel his coldness. He then expressed how I had hurt him, and how angry he was at me for not reaching out to him while he was dealing so intensively with his father's death and his problematic family.

I felt terrible... and surprised! Terrible because I knew immediately that he was right—I should have reached out. Surprised because I was following how I understood the rules and expectations of my professional training. I also assumed, because he was in training as a psychotherapist, that he would appreciate my awkward and disappointing position. I was taught not to get involved *actually* with people's lives outside of the fifty minutes in the office where we *talked about* their lives and remained a distance from the realities of those lives. I explained this and how I deeply regretted his not having the opportunity to see and feel my true feelings of sadness and care for him during the acute period of his loss. I think he heard me, but nevertheless, he never returned to continue our work. I still feel terrible for the disappointment and hurt I caused him, and I still feel the pain I felt as he moved on from working with me.

In my prayer, I see Love looking compassionately at Nate as he tells the story of his disappointment in me and my hurting him. Love also is by Nate's side also looking at me with sadness as well as love. I share my sorrow and guilt as well as my desire to learn from this hurtful mistake.

Besides my prayer of sorrow and contrition for my neglect, I have tried to react to my guilt and regret in the best way anyone can. I learned from my mistake and acted differently in the future. My experience with Nate was one of the things that led me to have a more natural, more free, human, caring presence when I related to the people I worked with—an actual, active presence, in their actual lives, not just one talked about from a distance or experienced directly only in my office.

My emotionally wounding Nate helped me to learn not to underappreciate the importance and power of the actual relationships I formed with the people with whom I worked. However, even while highly valuing those relationships throughout my career, I still made hurtful decisions that led to guilt.

As an example, near the end of my career I worked with Kathy, who credited me with helping her positively transform her life. However, after a couple years and while we were still working together, she began to lose control of her physical health and misuse her psychiatric medications. She began to have more psychotic symptoms. Throughout our work together, I had wanted her to have more medical and psychiatric professionals on her support team, not only me. As she faced these new and very challenging difficulties, her career dreams crashed. She could no longer sustain her efforts to become and stay healthy. I insisted that she get more and different help than I could provide as a solo nonmedical practitioner.

We worked on moving her treatment from me to other professionals who were specialists in all the areas she acutely needed help in. As she procured that kind of help, I cut down on my meetings with

Kathy and eventually stopped working with her. She made it very clear that she did not want to stop her work with me, and she was upset with my insistence that we do so. As planned, after we stopped our work, I continued brief supportive phone contacts with her—external to her new treatment team—in order to reinforce my continuing caring presence and relationship in her life. Some months passed in this fashion.

One day, I learned that she had unexpectedly died just the day before. Since I was not part of her treatment team, I could not learn the details of her death. While I do not regret my decision to stop working together while continuing my support outside of official treatment, I do feel guilty about how painful it was for her to stop. Now, years later, I regularly bring this relationship to my prayer with Love. I try to see Love calling us both. Love wants to be with both of us, to know the range of feelings we each have, and to understand what happened. Love looks at us both with compassion. Love knows Kathy is more than her hurt and I am more than my hurtfulness.

OUR LIMITS IN PRAYER

It is common for us to pray imaginatively, holding others close in our minds and hearts. We often pray for others' healing and to help them meet challenges. We are interconnected with so many people in our lives, even vicariously through social media, that praying while holding others in our hearts is a natural and fundamentally human thing to do. For example, when we are in severe pain, say while awaiting surgery, it is human to be focused on ourselves and our own needs; it is also realistic, wholistic, to be aware of all the others we are related to in that moment—our surgeon, the nursing staff who will help prepare us and help us recover, and our friends and family who are powerless but for their hope and love. Love is simultaneously also calling all of them to greater relationship in prayer, giving them a chance to share their concerns for us, among all the other aspects of their lives.

Of course, in acute severe suffering we may not have the capacity to even think of prayer, for ourselves or for anyone else. Then we can hope that our suffering affectively communicates on its own without conscious intent. A groan, a cry, a surrender, all are expressive. And we hope others also cry out for us.

When we specifically consider guilt and regret, others are almost surely involved. We hurt people directly or indirectly. In our prayer, it is fitting that we bring to Love those we have hurt. In order not to speak for them, it is useful to imaginatively see them expressing their own experience to Love directly. Our focus is not on what they share, only that they are sharing. It is likely that we can't accurately imagine the content of what they would share, and we could be apprehensive about and disagree with what they might share.

I imaginatively see in my prayer that Nate and Kathy are also called by Love. I do not know whether they actually respond to Love or not. Nevertheless, I picture them with Love. I state my desire for that to Love. As Love looks at them warmly and with compassion, I imagine that they speak the details and feelings they are aware of and focused on. I cannot know what they say to Love, and I wouldn't be surprised if our stories conflicted in places. It is enough to know that Love is with them just as Love is with me. Again, Love sees them as more than their hurt and sees me as more than my hurtfulness.

Understandably, concern over accuracy and the facts can be part of the content of our prayer. What actually happened? Who is right? However, most essentially, prayer, truth, and Love are relationships.

Honesty matters in relationships, but isn't it the case that we typically learn the truth of ourselves gradually over time within the matrix of the developing loving relationships we have with ourselves, others, and Love?

Often when experiencing guilt, we pray or hope for forgiveness—from ourselves, Love, and those we hurt. Let's acknowledge here that forgiveness often does not take away the hurt in the other that we caused, and therefore it may not end our own suffering. Also, forgiveness often does not take away the pain that comes with learning about ourselves over time. Over time and with courage, we can learn things about ourselves related to our guilt. We can gain at least partial answers to questions such as: How could I not have seen beforehand how hurtful it would be to do what I did? What in me blinded me to the degree of hurt I actually caused? Besides the circumstances of the moment, what in me led me to that hurtful action or made me vulnerable to be so hurtful? What in me makes it difficult to admit I was responsible? And what in me makes it difficult to do my part to repair the damage? These are valuable things to learn even as they may be painful. Typically, we learn these things over time, and this is the major reason why our prayer with guilt may be repetitive and recur over years. We all have a lot to learn.

Here is the good news: We learn best as we experience that Love is with us. Yes, even as we learn how we are in fact guilty and how we are vulnerable to hurting others, we are loved. The whole of us is loved, not just the good parts, and not just the hurtful ones. And there's more good news: As we learn about our vulnerabilities, as we learn we are loved, we often become better attuned to Love. We develop and grow. The best sign of attunement is that we love more.

It is a blessing to be open to and see that Love simultaneously calls all of us, even the guilty. Likewise, Love is with all of us, wants to hear from all of us, and is listening to whatever any of us have to express, even our guilt. Love is a witness to our feelings, everyone's feelings, even those who see things differently than we do, even those who were hurt by us. Can we see the entire world is being called to prayer, greater relationship with each other, and greater relationship with Love? We are called to be open, to share, to listen, and gradually attune ourselves to Love.

IMAGINE AND PONDER

- The whole of us is loved, not just the good parts, and not just the hurtful ones. As we learn about our vulnerabilities, we often become better attuned to Love. The sign of attunement is that we love more, both ourselves and others.
- Can we see that Love calls everything, all, to greater relationship? This is the call to healing and wholeness.

CHAPTER 9

THE HELP REJECTOR AND THE CAREGIVER

(The Good Samaritan)

The stories in this chapter are for two sets of people: caregivers who are burning out or despairing because the person they are caring for is rejecting them and their help, and those persons cared for who are too wounded and angry to accept help.

The caregivers are strangers, friends, teachers, ministers, colleagues, parents, and spouses who are emotionally and physically depleted from the effort to care for very difficult, provocative, often angry and rejecting, wounded others. The caregivers continue to feel empathy toward these others. However, after a long while of caring, they have parts of themselves that wish they could quit their empathy and sense of responsibility. These parts are reciprocally angry and could reject the wounded ones. They want to be loving, but loving these wounded persons feels like too much—more than a full-time job, more like an all-encompassing career or vocation, even a new identity, or a loss of identity. They are broken with hurt and fear by these difficult persons whom they care about but who meanly critique or even reject them and their care time and time again.

The wounded and rejecting people live with a painful raw vulnerability that terrifies them. They attempt to protect that raw vulnerability by isolating themselves—often by aggressively pushing away caring others. They can't allow their vulnerability to be witnessed, touched, or commented on. They may long to be met and soothed and loved, but they cannot bear what always feels so rough, so little, insensitive, even teasing, and ultimately uncaring. They often hate themselves for being so angry and mean.

THE STORY OF THE GOOD SAMARITAN
(Luke 10:29-37)

A lawyer asks Jesus, "And who is my neighbor?" Jesus replies with a story of a traveler who was robbed, stripped, beaten, and left half-dead. A priest ventured by, saw the beaten man and passed on the opposite side of the road. Likewise, a Levite also saw the man and passed on the opposite side. However, a Samaritan traveler came upon him and was moved with compassion at the sight. He approached the victim, bandaged his wounds, put the man on his own animal, took him to an inn, and cared for him. The next day he gave money to the innkeeper to continue tending to the man's injuries. The Samaritan would return and pay the innkeeper whatever balance remained. When Jesus asks the lawyer which traveler was a neighbor to the victim, the reply is, "The one who treated him with mercy." Jesus said to the lawyer, "Go and do likewise."

THE TRANSFORMED STORY
(What happens next?)

Imagine you are sitting near Jesus as he teaches about loving one's neighbor. As he tells the story to answer the lawyer's question, you become acutely aware that it could apply to you but it is way too simple. Without intending to, you grumble aloud, "It's not that easy."

You have cared for many people, some strangers, and your question is this: What happens when you care about someone who rejects not only your care, but also you? You know some parents experience this with their adolescent and adult children. You understand why other people passed by the wounded man if they thought he might later be angry with and attack them for trying to help.

Alternatively, you may identify with the person rejected and broken by the side of the road. Your question is, what happens when you are helped in ways that make you feel afraid or that feel inadequate to your needs? You know what it is like to feel so in need and vulnerable that you are always warily on guard, ready to angrily push away people you perceive as threats. You have a sense that sometimes your defensive alarms can lead you to push away caring people, and you are often angry at yourself for doing so.

After he is finished with the lawyer, Jesus looks over the crowd. His eyes stop as he sees you and he seems to sense your agitation. You sense empathy in his eyes. He is waiting, seemingly inviting you to share your experience. You stand and continue the story that a moment ago seemed finished. You start off very slowly, in a staccato, controlled rhythm. It may not seem like it to the crowd around you, but you are carefully choosing words that get across what you want to express while also holding back the huge waves of feelings churning within your body. Each time another word escapes out into the air, you feel both more vulnerable and more rigid.

You say: "At the end of the week, the caregiver returns. The wounded person is stronger. Yet, something unexpected is occurring. The wounded person rages. The hate-filled tirades are directed toward the shocked and now frightened caregiver. The rageful victim is also spewing at the staff of the inn. More run to see what the ruckus is about. All of them are now uncomfortably and warily standing at a distance.

"The wounded one's rage focuses on the limitations of the caregiver's care and the limited treatment available at the inn. He is indignant that the caregiver *paid for someone else* to care and that the caregiver did not stay around longer to care personally and directly. He also is indignant that the caregiver's money bought only so much treatment, and the people he instructed to care only cared so much. The victim feels abandoned by the caregiver and staff. He devalues them all in a rage even as he remains in desperate need."

As you release that last word, you notice how tired you are and how you are able to take a full breath for the first time in a long time. You have been that tense and on edge. No one knows if you are the hated or the hateful of your story, the caregiver or the wounded one. The crowd is in an uncomfortable state of silence. Maybe their bodies are registering the tension you just released. You and Jesus, who clearly has welcomed your story with his eyes, are the only ones who seem to be breathing easily. He is present to you and compassionate no matter which person in the story you are.

This is the beginning of prayer, a relationship between you and Jesus. Maybe the others present will be moved to speak their related feelings and experiences too.

HELP-REJECTING SUFFERERS

Not everyone has had experiences like those in the transformed version of this Gospel story. If that is the case for you, say a prayer of thanksgiving right now. They are some of the most painful emotional experiences within relationships that one can have. Both people involved can feel the relationship is abusive.

Relationships like these are not uncommon. However, due to shame, they are often hidden from public view—that is, until the anger explodes publicly. They can occur between spouses or lovers, parents and children, siblings, colleagues at work, or bosses and employees. The wounds of the person rejecting help often cannot be seen, but they could be physical—for example, unrelenting chronic pain or addiction. They could also be more emotional—such as an intense conflict between fear and desire for closeness. Whether physical or emotional, the person rejecting help feels those wounds to be both shameful and raw, needing the highest degrees of vigilance for protection.

What is most hurtful and provocative to the caregiver is that the wounded person denies the reality of the caregiver, how the caregiver knows him or herself to be. Caregivers are told that they are not caring at all but that instead they are hurtful. These messages are conveyed with such intensity and action that it can feel to a caring empathic person that the attacks on their reality must have some accuracy to them—why else would someone attack so strongly? These experiences are often felt to be crazy-making, and they can naturally provoke in the caregiver angry defensive rebuttals that then can easily be seen by the wounded person as proof the caregiver isn't caring at all, but instead angry and hostile. The crazy-making experience just gets worse from there.

As an analogy, imagine someone you are trying to help grabbing your wrist strongly in public, shaking it, and saying with great anger, even hate, with ever-increasing volume, "Will you let go of me already? LET ME GO! NOW!" And that person is the one holding onto you! Tragically, you truly care about and are concerned for the person doing this to you. To have this happen once is frightening. To have this kind of interaction be an ongoing part of a relationship can be traumatic, leading you to be continually on guard in the relationship, not trusting, depleted, and avoidant. These interactions not only can provoke anger but also can end the relationship.

Simultaneously, the angry person who is in need of help actually does need help. That person hurts terribly and is also fearful that the help offered could hurt more than the original wound. Often the anger these people inflict on their caregivers is proportionate to the pain and need they feel. Their own hurt and their compensating ways of protecting themselves may have made them so sensitive, or they might be genetically predisposed to be so sensitive, that direct care may become counterproductive.

A CONTEMPORARY TRANSFORMATION

I had a close friend, Larry, who was emotionally wounded and related to me in the way I am describing here. Not surprisingly, we both felt the relationship was a source of suffering. There were long periods in which each of us stayed away from relating to the other because the pain and struggles were felt to be too hurtful.

Fortunately, with my wife Pam's encouragement, I was able to repeatedly bring this relationship with me into my prayer with Love. I must admit this was not easy to do. I so often wanted nothing to do with Larry, sometimes out of fear of his anger, sometimes because of my own anger and desire for retribution. I also was ashamed to bring such a mess to Love. My inadequacies in this relationship seemed so clear. I felt like a failure at caring, something at which I was supposed to be somewhat of an expert.

I always imagined Love was waiting for me compassionately. As I shared my suffering, I did not feel judgment, but relief. A kind of acceptance. I could feel Love was interested in having me share all my feelings, not just a summary of the two sides of the conflict with Larry, but my feelings of inadequacy and shame, my anger, my care, my wanting to quit the relationship, my feelings of hurt and rejection, my wanting to avoid the whole thing.

I knew I could not accurately represent Larry's feelings and experience to Love. What I felt strongly was that I didn't need to represent Larry. Love was not expecting me to analyze Larry, to be responsible for him, to get him right. Love was also not going to be a referee between us, a judge. I did have the feeling that Love would want to hear from Larry with the same fullness of feeling and experience. And Love would meet and be with Larry with the same compassion and acceptance that Love was gifting me. There was a wholeness to Love's vision and relating to Larry and me that I could only sense. I have not been able to live into it fully. However, for the last two years, Larry and I have had consistent and mostly positive contact. Our relationship is tentative, wary even. We each may hold back from putting much trust in the other, but I'm more willing to see where the relationship will go with Love.

This is what my own personal prayer has been like as I have prayed with the suffering embedded in my relationship with Larry. The image of Jesus willing to listen fully to whichever person would share, the Help

Rejector or the Caregiver, was useful in helping me bring the fullness of my personal version of that relationship to Love. Perhaps my experience in praying with such a painful and burdensome relationship will be useful to you in sharing your own difficult relationships with Love.

WHAT IS USEFUL IN THIS PRAYER

The most important element when praying about a problematic relationship is having positive foundational relationships. If we are going to continue to put ourselves in vulnerable relational positions, as caregiver or cared for, we need others who know and affirm us as we honestly know ourselves to be. In the contemporary story above, Pam was essential, not so much to spur me to keep in contact with Larry, although she did that, but to remind me of who I am, a caring person. I could recognize myself in how she related to me. She encouraged me to pray about the problematic relationship, and my prayer relationship worked the same way my relationship with Pam did. In my prayer, Love was interested in my experience. Love understood and was compassionate with me in my caring efforts and my hurt. I am certain Pam and Love are familiar with my faults, but they also know my strengths and intentions and values. I could only risk being hurt by Larry again and again because my resilience was reinforced by Love and loving relationships.

When praying about help-rejecting relationships, whether you are the helper or the rejector, ask for and look for people who will relate to you in ways within which you can recognize yourself honestly. Share with them your story within the problematic relationship and feel affirmed before you make the decision to take on more relational risk while feeling vulnerable to hurt and rejection.

IMAGINE AND PONDER

- We all have human limits to how loving we can be. We are responsible for protecting ourselves and those who love us from damaging relationships. Simultaneously discerning how to be attuned to both Love and our human limits is often not easy and often a part of our prayer.

CHAPTER 10

THE GOOD BUT GUILTY SHEPHERD

(The Parable of the Lost Sheep)

The following transformed story is for good people trying to do good in the world but whose actions bring about suffering and guilt. The parable of the lost sheep is transformed when someone (a shepherd) facing a difficult situation (a lost sheep) acts with good reason and intentions (finding the sheep), but there are unforeseen consequences and much suffering.

It is not uncommon for good people to suffer. However, this is a particular version in which someone actively does good, loves, and in the midst of those positive efforts other terrible things happen that could be the loving person's fault, or seen as if they are.

THE PARABLE OF THE LOST SHEEP (Luke 15:1-7)

In response to Pharisees criticizing Jesus because he welcomes and engages sinners, he imagines someone who loses one of a hundred sheep. That person leaves the ninety-nine and goes to find the lost one. He is joyful when he finds it, puts it on his shoulders, and returns home. He then calls his friends to rejoice with him because he found his lost sheep. He says that a sinner is like the lost sheep and the rejoicing is like heaven.

THE TRANSFORMED STORY
(What happens next?)

Imagine a crowd around Jesus, the teacher from Nazareth. A mixed crowd of tax collectors, sinners, Pharisees, lawyers, and curious good people with families. All of them seem to be listening closely, but there is some tension noticeable too. People are hearing the teacher's stories and messages differently, reacting differently, and they are not at all comfortable with each other. Various parts of the crowd at various moments during the teaching react with sounds of approval, others disapproval, and some with astonishment. When Jesus pauses, questions are shouted out and Jesus answers. He pauses often, his eyes meeting the eyes of individual listeners. They can tell he notices them, acknowledges their presence, holds them briefly in a moment.

A thin, unkempt man, dressed in patched, worn clothing, very slowly picks his way around people to get to the front. No one appears comfortable around him. He might smell—not just of the outdoors and smoky campfires, but of manure and sheep. Once he finds his place and looks up, he sees Jesus calmly, warmly gazing at him, almost as if he was being wordlessly welcomed. The man is respectful and listens.

During the story of the shepherd and the lost sheep, the man becomes somewhat agitated. He looks frustrated or impatient, and then, just like the others who questioned Jesus, he loudly says, "Teacher! Teacher! I have my own story, … and I want to hear your response." As Jesus comfortably looks into his eyes, he motions for the man to continue.

"I am, … or, that is, I was, until recently, … a shepherd." (At this revelation, the crowd seems united in their negative judgment of him.) He hesitates a moment, feeling the reactions around him, but he does not look around and is clearly intent on getting his story across to Jesus. He goes on, "My master knew me as honest and responsible, and he also could see, from the time I was a boy, that I loved sheep. They are so gentle, so innocent, and I cared for them as if they were family, my brothers and sisters, and I guess they were. I had no one else.

"Over time, my master rewarded me with the responsibility for a large flock. For the last three years I herded them from pasture to pasture in the proper seasons and protected them, not losing one. I knew each of them. One day, a few months ago, up in the hills over there, I noticed a sheep was missing. I settled the other sheep down in an area I knew, a space with lots of grass. It was protected, hidden amidst huge stones. I went off to find the sheep that I knew couldn't be too far away. Within an hour or so I had found it, and I was so happy. The sheep seemed happy too, or relieved." The crowd's murmuring seemed condescending to this description. "I put it around my neck, over my shoulders, and hurried back to the others."

Here the man stops. He is feeling something no one can make out. Jesus leans forward with concern. "Teacher, … the other sheep had been attacked. Wolves? Wild dogs? A few were injured, one was dead, and two were missing." During this last sentence, his voice breaks. He almost wails those last few words to get them out.

The crowd seems moved . . . by the suffering the animals endured and the agony that the shepherd portrays . . . at first. Then it can be sensed that they are beginning to turn against him, blame him.

The shepherd stands with his head down . . . in shame, . . . in grief, . . . and when he begins again, he is angry. It isn't directed at the crowd. No, it seems directed at Jesus. Jesus, who is still clearly moved by the shepherd's anguished story and is still holding the shepherd's whole body with his eyes.

The shepherd continues, "I loved those sheep. Each one. I am sure they each knew that. When necessary, I would search for each one of them in the same way to save them. Yet now I could see they were afraid. They didn't trust that I would protect them or could protect them." Even in his devastation, he seems to gather himself to say what is coming next. "When I returned to my master with the sheep that were left, a few carefully bandaged whom I myself alone pulled on a litter, my master beat me and banished me from his service."

His story is finished. He glares, unbowed, clearly not regretting anything, . . . and yet at the same time feeling so guilty and responsible, overcome by sorrow, grief, and loss. His anger is there, too, but confusing because now it is directed toward himself, his master, the crowd, and Jesus, all at once.

When he came to see and hear Jesus, a teacher he had only heard about, the shepherd didn't know that he would be moved to speak. But as he listened, he wanted to be known by Jesus. He wanted Jesus to know who he was, what happened to him, and what he was feeling. He was a loving man. He knew what Jesus was talking about from his own experience. Yet even while being so attuned, his life had changed terribly in an instant.

He could see the compassion and interest in the face of Jesus. Jesus did know him. The shepherd also somehow was aware that his was a story his community should hear too. There would be those who knew his master, there would be those who loved sheep, there would be those who identified with his responsibilities and love, those who looked down upon him, and those who judged him.

He told his story, unexpectedly, publicly. He laid it all out before Jesus and the crowd.

Everyone now looked to Jesus. Everyone saw his compassion.

A CONTEMPORARY TRANSFORMATION

The following story is an amalgam of my experience with my parents' dying, Pam's (my wife's) experience with her mother's dying, and our experience with a dying friend in his nineties.

Jerry's mother was ninety-six years old. Years ago, he had been designated by her to serve as her medical power of attorney if needed. Now he was needed in that role. She was unconscious, in the hospital, and there was a decision to be made by Jerry between, on the one hand, an easily performed procedure that would solve the acute cause of her being hospitalized and, on the other hand, palliative care and hospice. That choice was being considered because the recovery from the surgery would probably require months of pain and discomfort in bed with no guarantees that she would be able to regain anywhere near the level of functioning she had prior to this sudden illness. Jerry knew his mother did not want extreme lifesaving measures, and recently she had made it clear to him that she did not even want lifesaving surgery at this point in her life. She said she loved her life, all of it until now, and asked how much time would it give her anyway at age ninety-six. Even before this latest hospitalization, it was clear to her that her life was declining as it should, and she thought about what her quality of life would be after almost any kind of surgery at her age.

His brother and sister wanted him to respect their mother's wishes and have her referred to palliative care and hospice. They loved her as he did, but he was leaning toward her having the surgical procedure because it "normally" would have been such a routine intervention and recovery—that is, with someone twenty or more years younger. And, of course, there was always a chance that her recovery would be quite manageable. The medical professionals did not have clear answers for him, they were split in their opinions like he and his siblings were.

He wanted her to have a chance at more good life. He thought she would appreciate it and be grateful. He decided for his mother having the surgery.

It went well.

Within days, however, his mother was suffering with an opportunistic infection. The medical people seemed to get it under control and they sent her home. She was seriously uncomfortable even with in-home nursing care. She was not happy. Her spirits and energy were taxed to their limits. His siblings were trying to make the best of the situation and be supportive of their mother, but anyone could see she was suffering. Within a month of the surgery, she was readmitted to the hospital, again unconscious. The same problem that had put her there before had returned in a new area. She would need another similar surgery to live.

This time, his brother and sister were adamant in their opinions. He understood their anger at his continued reluctance to refer his mother to hospice. He felt guilty about his first decision, but he also felt he had made it with the best of intentions. Now he was dimly aware that he might be wanting to stick with the same decision again in order to justify himself, . . . maybe this time the result would be what he had first hoped and everyone would be happy for the way it all worked out.

One night he was sitting quietly by his mother's hospital bed. This was after he had argued with his brother and sister in a corner of her room and a nurse had to intervene telling them that their mother just might be hearing them. The nurse said they needed to begin again trying to be attuned with what was best for their mother given her whole life. Almost impetuously as he remembered the nurse's words, he went to find the hospital's chapel.

He found it without much difficulty. It was inter-religious. All the other times he had been visiting in the hospital or meeting with staff, he had not given any thought to the chapel. He did remember the signs pointing out its direction. That night he stood just within the doors. He needed time to get accustomed to the dark, though he immediately appreciated the quiet that he could feel was already working to calm him. Well, maybe not calm him, but focus him. He found a seat, in a corner, in the dark, and began laying out, not quite whispering, all that had been happening, all that he felt and thought, how he was trying his best to be a good shepherd to his mother. His mother's presence was strong. So was the presence of his brother and sister.

He was beginning to pray.

PRAYER AS CALL AND RESPONSE

Prayer is the call and response with Love within relationships.

Notice in the transformed Gospel story that there is space for the shepherd. Jesus is waiting, welcoming, ready to listen, available, and present. The shepherd comes into the space, takes up space, and is a meaningful presence to Jesus.

Jesus could be seen as inviting, even as somehow having called the suffering shepherd. It could also be that the shepherd's longing for loving understanding and care led the shepherd on. It is like when you take a new phone or computer out of the box and turn it on. There is something already inside placed there by the manufacturer that tries to find a compatible network to connect to, and there is a network always on the lookout for compatible devices. It is like a plant that has a built-in need for the sun and searches for it, while the sun's light and warmth actively call for the plant's cells to respond.

In my more contemporary version, it could be that the nurse who broke up the siblings' arguing recalled for them the most important value in the moment, the well-being of their mother, and perhaps that recall helped Jerry feel and respond to the call to the chapel.

Once in each other's presence, the shepherd begins to share with Jesus. In the chapel, Jerry begins to share with Love. Their stories come out in all their detail with all their feeling. See and feel the shepherd and Jerry being listened to closely, empathically.

Notice in both the transformed Gospel and the contemporary version that there is a community, a family, other people around. They, too, are being called and invited to respond, invited to be like Jesus and listen to the shepherd's own story, or invited to hear Jerry's story. In addition, they are being called to share with Love their own perspectives on the shepherd and the shepherd's sheep, or Jerry and his care of his mother.

Can you feel there is some sense that the shepherd's community needs healing, not just the shepherd? Similarly, can you feel Jerry's family needs healing, not just Jerry and his mother? These invitations challenge us to build a greater sense of community and mutual belonging. Love wants to hear and relate to us all. We all are called to relate to Love and each other, the lost shepherd and his neighbors, Jerry and his family.

I mentioned in the introduction to this book how my own ninety-eight-year-old mother is in hospice. As I write this, there is no clear acute physical process that will lead to her death. However, her slow decline is relentless. I try to be a loving good shepherd for my mother, and yet there are decisions I have faced and will face where the best choice is difficult for me to discern, even with frequent prayer. I dread making a decision that will lead to greater suffering for her. In addition, while my two brothers are also lovingly caring for my mother, at times we have had heated conflicts over how best to love her as she approaches death. My decisions could harm my relationships with my brothers.

Over these last three years, Love has been a compassionate companion wanting relationship with me, wanting to hear and accept my feelings, trying to help me remain attuned to my love for my mother and my brothers and to be a good shepherd. As Love knows, being a good shepherd is not an easy job. Fortunately, I have been blessed with people in my community, like Pam and my friends, who have helped sustain me. We all are called to be that supportive community for those trying to be good shepherds in the midst of life's many challenges.

Most relationships have an aspect of prayer to them, loving calls and responses. The cries for interest, understanding, and help are often obvious. Sometimes they may be more hidden, protecting fear, embarrassment, or shame. All relationships, families, and communities have a role in becoming aware of and attuned to Love as part of Love's ongoing response to prayer. We are the primary means Love has of responding to our prayer and the prayers of others.

IMAGINE AND PONDER

- Most relationships have an aspect of prayer to them—calls and responses hoping for more engagement, relationship, and love.

CHAPTER 11

SYSTEMATIC OPPRESSION

(The Centurion and His Servant and The Canaanite Woman)

No one, not even Jesus, can be born into this world without being affected by and participating more or less in the "powers, dominions, and principalities" of this world. Remember, for example, how Jesus was a central figure in the slaughter of the Holy Innocents. As an infant, he had no awareness or choice in that situation. In other situations, however, Jesus—like all of us—had more or less awareness and more or less choice. In the following two transformed Gospel stories, Jesus reinforces or participates in systematic oppression. We might say that most humans are, at various times and degrees, simultaneously agents and victims of various systems of oppression. When praying in these situations, one could pray with the painful feelings of the oppressed or with the awareness and feelings of guilt of the oppressor.

THE HEALING OF A CENTURION'S SERVANT
(Matthew 8:5-13; see also Luke 7:1-10 and a variation in John 4:46-54)

A military commander approached Jesus. He said his servant was paralyzed and suffering terribly. Jesus said he would come and cure the servant. The commander replied, "Lord, I am not worthy to have you enter under my roof; only say the word and my servant will be healed." Jesus praised his faith and said his servant was healed.

A TRANSFORMED STORY
(What happens next?)

Imagine the centurion is visibly touched by how Jesus treated him. He is still there, to the side of the crowd, as they all receive the news that his servant is healed. The crowd is amazed but disturbed. Some are obviously angry. Jesus senses and hears these rising feelings among his followers, his own people. He turns to them, opening his arms, and invites them all to sit with him. He looks at them compassionately and with love as they settle, and then he nods, inviting them to tell their stories and share their feelings.

One woman stands and is so upset that she cries to him, "That man's soldiers chased and killed my son. Witnesses say my boy was just running and playing with his friends. The soldiers said he stole something and then the group was throwing stones at the soldiers. Lies! And that one," now pointing at the centurion, "supported his soldiers. My son is dead. How could you heal his servant?" She falls to the ground, sobbing. A man yells, "How could you heal this man's servant, doing something good for this man, when he exploits us, harms your own people, each day, imprisoning us in our own land, unjustly taking advantage of my family and yours, doing damage to our bodies and spirits." Others speak up as well, bravely, considering the centurion's presence and power.

Jesus is moved and cries with them. He knows what they are saying is true. This man, this commander, is an active part of their oppression. Jesus easily sees how his own healing actions reinforce the oppressor. The centurion witnesses all of this. Jesus and he hold each other's gaze for a long time. Their eyes are brimming with compassion for each other, and also for the suffering of the crowd. The crowd witnesses this. Perhaps Jesus's kindness undermines the oppressor. Jesus knows that grace and mercy are gifts that none of us earn.

This is prayer developing, relationships developing.

A SECOND GOSPEL STORY, THE CANAANITE WOMAN

(Matthew 15:21-28, see also Mark 7:24-30)

A Canaanite woman called out to Jesus for pity and for her daughter who was tormented by a demon. He did not respond to her. She harassed his followers for a response, and they told Jesus to send her away. He told them he was sent only to help those from the house of Israel. She came to him directly then, saying, "Help me." He replied just as directly to her, "It is not right to take the food of the children and throw it to the dogs." She responded, "Please, Lord, for even the dogs eat the scraps that fall from the table of their masters." He remarked on her great faith and said her request was granted. Her daughter was healed in that moment.

THE SECOND GOSPEL STORY TRANSFORMED
(What happens later?)

This transformed story continues the Gospel version. Imagine: the next day there is a group of Canaanites waiting by the side of the road for Jesus and his followers. His own people become anxious. Everyone with him, but not Jesus, slows as they come near the Canaanites. His people are tensing for a confrontation. When Jesus is close to the Canaanites, he stops, and his eyes meet the eyes of each person there. He silently invites them to sit with him off the road where there is some shade and a breeze. He motions for them to speak. He wants to hear what they have to say, and they can see his interest and desire in his eyes and gestures.

A man, in fact the husband of the woman who begged him the day before, stands and speaks first. He begins loudly, saying, "So we are dogs!" And he looks around at his proud people. "We are dogs?" His anger rises with his voice. "And you cure one of us because another barks and barks and outmaneuvers your ways of pushing her away." He almost spits. "If I didn't love my daughter so much and want the best for her, I would return the scraps from your table. You humiliate, then you give a blessing. You pet my wife with your words, and send her off. You humiliate us again and more. How am I to thank you for that? Are we to continue to be devalued and beg? We are different, we are grateful, and we have needs. Do you not have eyes to see? Yet you were treated with respect by my wife, and here we are, angry, but speaking to you with respect."

They can see Jesus listening. They can see him being touched by this husband just like he was touched by his wife the day before. He feels the truth in what her husband says just as he felt the truth in what she said. He looks on them all with love.

This is prayer developing, relationships developing.

PRAYING WITH OPPRESSION

It is worth remembering here that Jesus knows oppression, and the painful feelings that come with it, from being the victim of it as part of an occupied society, and, as we see in the above stories, from the perspective of reinforcing it. While his actions may have undermined oppression to some degree, we know that kindness and mercy often do not always, quickly, or easily transform the chronicity of injustice. We can imagine Jesus waiting empathically for us to share the similarly painful feelings that we ourselves have of being both oppressed and contributing to oppression. Of course, as always, your prayer comes from your own personal feelings and experience, so you might just focus on the part of oppression most painful to you in this moment. Share with Jesus using the framework of the transformed Gospel stories above, or use them as a jumping-off point to share your own story directly.

A CONTEMPORARY TRANSFORMATION

Since I am an old white privileged male, it is a rare occasion when, in my prayer, I feel justified in taking the position of a member of an oppressed group and identifying with someone like the Canaanite woman in the Gospel story. I included her story and its transformation above mostly to offer one model for praying for those who do suffer while being a member of an oppressed group in our society due to race, gender, socio-economic status, immigration status, sexuality, or other scapegoating factor.

I personally have used the transformed Gospel story of the Canaanite to pray with the suffering that comes with my having limitations that lead me to painfully contribute to oppression. What follows is one example. It goes a bit further into my experience with Darrell Jones, whom I already introduced in chapter 5 and its discussion of the suffering of the Holy Innocents and their families.

I couldn't help but notice how frequently the Canaanite woman had to deal with "NO" coming from Jesus's disciples and Jesus himself. As the transformed story makes clear, these are the NOs of systematic oppression—No, you can't; No, don't; No, go away; No, you don't deserve; and I don't care, No.

One day, while talking with my spiritual director of many years, a Jesuit Catholic priest and a clinical psychologist, William Barry, SJ, I was told that there was a man in prison who wanted to talk with a psychologist outside the prison system, a psychologist he hoped to trust. Feeling like this was a roundabout way of asking if I would be that psychologist, I basically said, "No."

Bill tried again maybe a month or two later. He said a little more about the person, that he was in prison for murder. I was too busy. Since the prison was forty-five minutes away, I didn't have the time to drive out, visit, and then return. I said no again.

Yet another time, Bill said that he himself talked to the man regularly. I said I had virtually no experience with prisons, let alone prisoners, and no experience with violent persons. I was building to my third no. He said that this man said he was innocent. He also said that he talked to the man by phone. He added that he thought it would be a short-term intervention.

I said OK.

After many months, I had another set of chances to say no and the impulses to follow through on them. They came the first time I talked with Darrell on the phone. It took that long for Darrell himself to arrange with the warden to allow him to have private, non-recorded telephone calls with an outside therapist. I can't begin to tell you how unusual these things are: to have an outside therapist and to have non-recorded calls. This was a super-max security prison with hundreds of inmates. I see now that I should have seen all this as a sign of how difficult it is to say no to Darrell. Even the warden had difficulty. I was having my own contemporary experience of what the disciples and Jesus were in for in talking with the Canaanite woman.

Three times during that first phone call, spontaneously, unexpectedly I heard an inner voice saying to me each time, "I don't want this to change my life; I don't want this to change my life; I don't want this to change my life." The three times that happened during the phone call were my opportunities to say no. I might have said something like, "You know, Darrell, I don't think this is going to work out. I am not the right person to do this with you." Instead, I became tearful each time it happened, and I tried to hold back the tears so my crying wouldn't be noticeable to Darrell over the phone.

What I have thought for a long time is that these cries of mine, "I don't want this to change my life," were cries to Love. They were my crying out in prayer. I was answering a call from Love to love Darrell. But I also was trying to limit my response to the call, limit my vulnerability, trying to negotiate the terms. My feelings wanted me to say to Love something like, "OK, I'll talk with this man and try to be useful, but I don't want this to change my life."

Well, it did change my life. My talking with Darrell was no short-term therapeutic intervention. It became a relationship that is ongoing for over ten years.

THE RICHNESS OF PRAYER

What is fascinating to me is that at no time did I feel Love judging me. Love could have negatively judged me for saying no, for refusing to become involved. Love could have judged me for being part of the mostly silent *Commonwealth of Massachusetts v. Darrell Jones*. I could judge myself as selfish, or as negatively influenced by a prejudice against prisoners, but I never felt those things while talking to Darrell, and I never felt those judgments of myself in my prayer.

What did happen? I felt compassion and support. I did something hard for me, changed my stable life, opened it up to another, a very different other, eventually many others as it turned out, and to much painful learning about our criminal justice (and too often unjust) system. Mostly I felt Love's support through Pam and my friends with whom I shared my challenges.

I came to see that involving my friends in my challenges and developing a relationship with Darrell was integral to my prayer. It was Darrell, maybe the voice of Love in that moment, who encouraged me to get others involved in the fight for justice for wrongly incarcerated people. My stories of Darrell challenged them too. Simultaneously, their support of me and eventually Darrell was Love responding to prayer, Love working with us. I imagine Jesus's challenging interaction with the Canaanite woman led Jesus to challenge his followers to become more supportive of him and each other as they all became more open to and probably more affirming of her people.

From that first phone call so many years ago, my relationship with Darrell began to shift my felt experience and understanding of what it is to be in prison; to be falsely, unjustly accused, convicted, and imprisoned when innocent; to have thirty-two years of your life purposefully stolen; to have people try to actively break your spirit and your will; to be imprisoned with the purposeful expectation of others that you will die there; to be obligated to do more for justice, learn from experience, share my learning, and act accordingly socially and politically; and to have another black friend with his own wonderful black friends and family for me to meet and befriend.

The change has been immense. It has also been a blessing. Maybe Jesus felt similarly when he finally said yes to the Canaanite woman. My praying with her suffering with Jesus helped me become a positive part of Darrell's life and Darrell such a positive part of mine.

Love encourages learning and growth. We slowly move in the direction of openness, expansiveness, and wholeness. Love brings more relationship, more love into our lives, by our being loved more and being more loving. These are the things that praying and relating to Love around Darrell brought into my life. These are the things to be on the lookout for in your own life as you pray.

IMAGINE AND PONDER

- Sometimes we contribute to others' oppression because we are afraid to change, to disrupt our lives, and we miss out on responding to Love's call to witness to the truth and to love more.
- Love does not harshly judge or condemn us. Love loves us unconditionally, AND Love persistently calls us to become more of our best selves, to witness to the truth, to love more.
- We often feel Love's support and compassion through friends, family, and the kindness of strangers. We often help others feel Love by the support and compassion we offer family, friends, and others, even strangers.

CHAPTER 12

ILLNESS AND DEATH RETURN

(The Cure of the Man at the Pool and The Raising of Lazarus)

These are stories for those of us whose suffering returns after it has receded, gone into remission, or even vanished completely. These stories try to hold the disappointment, fear, frustration, disillusionment, anger, and perhaps even despair that may come with these returns in our lives.

THE CURE OF THE MAN AT THE POOL (John 5:1-18)

Near the gate where animals were brought into the Temple in Jerusalem, there was a pool associated with healing. Many ill, blind, and physically limited people lay there. When the water in the pool was stirred, it was believed to have the power to heal. Jesus saw one ill man who had been there thirty-eight years. The man told Jesus that he wanted to be well, but there was no one to bring him to the pool soon enough once the water was stirred. Jesus said to him, "Rise, take up your mat, and walk." The man immediately became well.

THE TRANSFORMED STORY
(What happens later?)

Thirty-eight years of illness! After the man at the pool was made well, I imagine it took him many months to even begin to adjust to living in the world outside of the Temple. He was frightened and anxious during that period. Only gradually did he find a place to live, make friends, give up begging, and find a job. Later, as he was developing a romantic relationship for the first time in his life, with a widow who learned and appreciated his story, he became quite ill and incapacitated. He once again remained ill for years. He lost his job and had to move. His wife and friends, however, remained with him.

He learned of Jesus's death not long after it occurred. He heard how the number of Jesus's followers kept increasing after his death. Before the man's second illness, despite his period of anxiety after being cured, he often prayed with great gratitude. With the onset of his second illness, however, he was too discouraged, scared, and even angry to pray. His wife prayed for him. She prayed for another miracle cure. None occurred.

Very gradually, his memory of Jesus looking at him with love and helping him years before returned. One night, unable to sleep due to pain, he began in his imagination to tell Jesus what he had experienced and felt since Jesus actively sought him out and cured him. He described his fears and challenges, what he was thankful for, and now his continuing pain, suffering, and, at times, despair. He shared his anger at additional years of suffering beyond the thirty-eight years in the Temple. He felt the respite of a few years was like a tease. He imagined Jesus listening to him just as Jesus had years before within the Temple grounds. He was responding within his relationship with Jesus. He was consciously praying.

A SECOND GOSPEL STORY: THE RAISING OF LAZARUS (John 11:1-44)

Lazarus, Mary, and Martha were siblings. Jesus loved them. When Lazarus was fatally ill, the sisters sent a message to Jesus. He waited two days, during which he knew that Lazarus had died. He told his followers that they would go to Lazarus and Jesus would awaken him from his sleep. When Jesus arrived, Lazarus had been in his tomb four days. Martha and Mary separately and directly told him that they believed he had a role in Lazarus's death, that their brother would not have died if Jesus had been there. Mary wept at Jesus's feet, and then he had them bring him to the tomb. There Jesus wept too. Those who witnessed his tears, witnessed his love for Lazarus. Jesus had the stone sealing the tomb rolled away, prayed to his Father, and then loudly cried out, "Lazarus, come out!" He did come out, tied, and his face was wrapped in cloth. Jesus said to free him.

THE SECOND TRANSFORMED STORY (What happens later?)

After Jesus brought him back from the dead, Lazarus lived with his two sisters. Imagine all three loved and missed Jesus, who was tortured and executed not long after he raised Lazarus. Then Lazarus became ill and suffered. He died once again. His sisters were indeed thankful for the additional time they had been given with Lazarus, but they still grieved deeply for many months after his death. They once again felt anger at Jesus. Why raise Lazarus just to have him suffer and die again? To them it sometimes felt like a cruel joke.

When they remembered Jesus's love for Lazarus and themselves, and Jesus's tears at Lazarus's tomb, they felt like Jesus wanted once again to hear their experiences and feelings. Imagining Jesus, they shared their gratitude and grief and anger. They were responding again within their relationship with Jesus. They were praying consciously.

A CONTEMPORARY TRANSFORMATION

Well over a decade ago, my cousin Pete, whom I grew up with, was very seriously ill for months and months. He was in and out of hospitals with lengthy stays. Cousin Pete lived alone, not far from me, without immediate family nearby. I was his health-care proxy. While mutual friends were involved, much of the day-to-day management of his care was my responsibility. It was a traumatic time for both of us. I was afraid Pete would die or be incapacitated in some way for years to come.

During the acute phases of his illness, I was not only afraid that I would not be able to take good enough care of him physically but also that I would not take good enough care of what was previously his stable life. I had images of his life falling apart. I worried about his finances, getting him food, and his house disintegrating around him.

There were two scripture passages that focused my prayer day after day. One was the Twenty-Third Psalm, which begins, "The Lord is my shepherd, there is nothing I lack." I didn't know whether I could be a good, effective shepherd to Cousin Pete's very ill sheep. I felt I lacked so much of what I needed. Pete had always been able to take care of himself. If one of us needed significant help in some way, we talked over the options together and came to a consensus on how to proceed. I would have said, when needed, that we shepherded together as a team. When Pete became ill, he often wasn't able to consult with me, let alone co-shepherd. I felt very alone at times and overwhelmed with my responsibility for a very ill sheep. I prayed continually that Love would shepherd us both. For many months the situation worsened.

Given those feelings of aloneness and overwhelm, the Gospel story I prayed most often with was the one I used in chapter 1—Jesus calming the storm. I transformed and reimagined it many different ways as the months passed with so much uncertainty regarding Cousin Pete's health and my self-doubt. What fit my ongoing feelings and situation most often was some variation in which Pete and I were in the boat with Jesus and a few of our friends. The huge storm did not let up for days, weeks, even months. It was full of dangers for Pete and there were some for me as well. In fact, what I imagined in my prayer fit our actual situation in another way I felt to be symbolic: I can't swim!

Jesus often seemed asleep. Just as often, I tried to wake him—not always successfully. When he was awake, I let him know day after day what I was experiencing, what I knew of Pete's experience, what we both felt, what I feared, how angry I was, what I desired, how close I was to despair, how much Pete and our relationship meant to me, how much he and I needed help of all kinds. I was responding within my relationship with Love.

ONGOING FEAR AND GRATITUDE IN PRAYER

Once Cousin Pete's health began to get a bit better, there was much for which I was thankful. In fact, I imagined throwing a big party to celebrate his wellness and specifically to thank our friends who had helped shepherd and navigate us through the acute phases of his illness. However, Pete's illness improved only gradually, over years, and never completely disappeared. It still remains in significant ways. In addition, my fear and vigilance remain. They are reawakened whenever Pete experiences something that reminds me of the fact that he could become ill like that again. In those circumstances, I have intense unfocused anxiety that makes it difficult to concentrate or sleep, flashbacks of being powerless to help, and catastrophic fears of what other bad things might happen. His illness was never completely and forever cured. I have never felt we were distant enough from his traumatic illness or my own related trauma to celebrate.

I am thankful for the many ways Pete is better, for how I was a good-enough co-shepherd with others and Love, for our supportive friends who helped us navigate the storm we faced, and for how our friendship has been blessed with new people whom I met and became friends with during his illness. I share these positive experiences and feelings with Love just as I share my traumatic feelings and experiences that remain within me. I feel Love continues to desire to hear it all. We continue in loving relationship, in prayer.

Pain and suffering are often not cured once and for all. That reality brings with it sadness and anger, dissatisfaction and fear. Yet, in the midst of that pain and suffering, our continuing relationship with Love remains available. Over time, that relationship may lead to consolation, reasons to be grateful, and a sense of wholeness. The wholeness comes, in part, with accepting the negative and the positive, but mostly it comes from attuning ourselves and our efforts to the ever-present possibility of more and deeper intimacy and love in our lives.

IMAGINE AND PONDER

- Healing and wholeness come, in part, with accepting the negative and the positive within our lives, but mostly healing and wholeness come from attuning ourselves and our efforts to the ever-present possibility of more and deeper intimacy and love in our lives.

CHAPTER 13

MISOGYNY

(A Woman Caught in Adultery)

This is another story of oppression. In this case, it is society's scapegoating of women. It is concerned less with privilege and patriarchy, and more with the feelings of vulnerability that we all have and would do well to be become more attuned to and care for.

A WOMAN CAUGHT IN ADULTERY
(John 8:2-11)

It was early in the morning and Jesus was already teaching in the Temple. The religious leaders brought to him a woman caught in adultery. They told him the punishment was stoning, and they wanted to know what he thought. Jesus began writing on the ground with his finger. They continued to pressure him. He stood up and said, "Let the one among you who is without sin be the first to throw a stone at her." He then crouched and continued writing. One by one they went away. Soon, he was alone with the woman. He asked, "Has no one condemned you?" She replied, "No." He said, "Neither do I condemn you."

THE TRANSFORMED STORY
(What else is happening? What occurs later?)

Imagine Jesus could tell as the morning progressed that other people with a different kind of energy were joining the crowd around him. The intimacy of the group was changing to something more like a spectacle. Many of the people he was teaching in the morning began walking away as the mood of the group began to change.

Of course, everyone heard what had happened. An adulterer had been caught in the very act. Judgment would be certain, quick, and clear, as would the execution. Many felt that society needed these kinds of consequences to repair the hurt and disruption that adultery caused to the civil order.

Yes, there was judgment, a solution, and order, but justice? Where was justice?

"Where are you going?" Ann asked. Her husband, David, had been rushing around in a preoccupied way. It might have been furtively. It might have been excitedly. It was difficult to tell. She was beginning to feel vulnerable.

Not stopping his activity, David said, "To stone an adulterer if you must know."

"Oh, a man?"

"Of course not!" And he left.

Ann and David were uncomfortable and unsettled. This scenario was being repeated throughout the town with more or less those same feelings. The vulnerability on the one side and the guilt on the other were rarely explicit. Some couples stayed home until they thought the disturbing events would be over—the inequality, the scapegoating of women, the killing disturbed them. Perhaps there were women who came to listen and observe, witnesses to oppression, on the edges of the crowd of mostly men. Maybe there were also a few women at the front of the crowd who were actively fueling the indignant fire within the men.

I imagine Jesus could feel the tension in the individuals and the couples, and among all the men and the women in the entire town. In this moment, his focus was not the woman on trial, the power of the crowd, or the focus on him by the ringleaders who were using this not-uncommon moment to trap and ultimately condemn him too. He looked at each face, each body, each set of eyes that glanced his way. To him, the crowd didn't hide the individuals. To him, the crowd didn't cloak the tension in those persons, those couples, their marriages, the underlying tensions between all men and women in the town. He felt compassion for each, all the women and all the men. There was suffering in all of them, trauma, if truth be told, from the long history of men treating women in these scapegoating ways. If the trauma wasn't felt consciously by each of them, it was available in the air around them to be taken in. It was having effects through the tension in their bodies, individually and collectively.

Awareness and empathy are not qualities of a mass of people. They are not qualities of people whose traumas are activated. Fear, anger, and scapegoating can harden one to sensitivity, empathy, care, and love. A crowd can easily numb the sensitivity within the individuals that comprise it.

When Jesus was asked about her sentencing, the crowd wondered what he would say. They tried to decipher what he was writing. Could it be that, after he looked into their eyes, his writing was a way to refocus them and quiet them? A quiet, waiting mass of people might become more of a collection of individuals, and therefore perhaps a bit more open and attentive. It could be that in waiting for him and trying to decipher him, trying to see what he was thinking and feeling, they were, simultaneously and without knowing it, looking into themselves more.

It could be that he was writing a passage from scripture that they all were familiar with, when King David in a fury demands that the prophet, Samuel, tell him who the guilty one is so that he can be punished. Samuel says to David, "That man is you." A declaration that echoes within every individual and generation.

When Jesus did look up to speak, he was looking again into the eyes of each of them, one at a time, and he spoke to their discomfort and their guilt, but not with judgment. His purpose was to help heal them, all of them, by addressing the reality of men and women. They were all vulnerable. They all had been hurt and could be hurtful. They were all equally respected and loved by God, a part of the whole, each belonging. With only a few words, Jesus enacted an astonishing countercultural shift within the crowd, from harsh merciless judgment to acceptance and some degree of identification. It may have only been temporary, but nevertheless it was a dramatic illustration of what is possible.

After the crowd dispersed and he spoke to the woman, the scapegoat of that crowd, and she left, he sat there and continued to write in the dirt. Picture that slowly, for the rest of the day, individuals from the crowd returned and approached him as if they were called. They began to share with him the discomfort in their hearts about how they saw and what they felt about their relationships with women and men. In addition to intense anger and fear, they spoke of loss, how they felt vulnerable, and where they might feel responsible. Some of those who had stayed in their homes waiting for these events to pass came to talk with him as well. They shared shame, of not knowing what to do, of being fearful of how they would be judged, of not living up to their best selves or what they thought was right.

He listened with love to each one and felt love for all. This was the beginning of prayer and relationship for each one who responded to him and indirectly for their community.

In his heart, he wondered if any of them would seek out the scapegoated woman to talk with and perhaps make amends to. He wondered how she might respond.

Late in the evening, the scapegoated woman and one of the women who had been adding to the crowd's foment returned to find him. They told him what they shared with each other. This was the beginning of prayer too.

A year later, the scapegoated woman was living in a different town. She secretly had received money from some of the people in the city to help her move.

In her new town, she was respected by the people she lived and worked among. She was often acutely lonely, but not too unhappy. When she heard that Jesus was tortured and executed, she was not surprised. She cried deeply and mourned his death, remembering how he treated her, how he saved her.

She often remembered how he looked at her with love. In these moments she would also imagine speaking to him, letting him know what her life was like and all the feelings she had—the fears, the hopes, what she was angry at, what she was thankful for, what she was unhappy about, and how lonely she was. She also often pictured him quiet, writing in the dirt, while she waited silently—fearful and hopeful.

A CONTEMPORARY TRANSFORMATION

One of the many blessings and honors of being a psychotherapist for so many years was hearing and learning the intimate stories of people whose experiences were different from mine. Most often, they were women's stories—of inequality, unshared or unequal responsibility, shaming, exclusion, and scapegoating. I could almost always find an event or pattern in my own history that would let me empathically link and feel into any experience of theirs, except one. I don't think I ever succeeded in being able to get an accurate experiential felt sense of the continual vulnerability that women can feel, a vulnerability that is available to be consciously felt at any moment, a vulnerability to devaluation and danger. Other devalued and oppressed groups know what it is like to live that way, to have reason to be wary all the time.

One of my profound learnings about women's vulnerability and devaluation is that it is so culturally ingrained that it often goes unidentified as a powerful factor in anxiety, anger, impulsive behavior, depression, and addiction.

I remember Susan, who grew up with a sister, two brothers, and two loving parents. She came to psychotherapy with me, longing for a long-term passionate love relationship with a man and simultaneously fearful of marriage and having children. When she and her siblings were growing up, her brothers had pushed their parents' boundaries in various ways, dated and had sex as teenagers, went to college, quickly married, and had children. Susan and her sister didn't. They were careful to please their parents. As teens they were very conflicted about their bodies and sexuality. Though quite smart and better in school than their brothers, they had to make a case to their parents to go to top colleges. They eventually had love relationships and some sexual experience that they hid even as adults from their parents. None of the relationships lasted.

Susan suffered with profound loneliness as well as self-doubt and anger. She had a prayer relationship with God in which she pleaded for what she needed in her life. She couldn't understand how Love wouldn't respond positively, while she felt at the same time there must be something wrong with her.

It took a long time for Susan to feel she was loveable in Love's eyes. The positive therapeutic relationship she had with me contributed to that learning. It also took time for her to understand that much of her anger was about how she and many other women had grown up feeling fearful, often being unfairly treated. Over time, her prayer became silent. Not pleading for what she had missed and still desired, yet not accepting of the status quo. Without words, she placed herself in Love's healing presence, available for the relationship with a man that she wanted while also being fearful, assertive, brave, indignant, hopeful, and more and more herself.

VULNERABILITY AND TRUST IN PRAYER

There are so many ways we are vulnerable in our lives and not in control, so many ways forces actively seem to work against us. A ready example of undermining forces are the intense expectations our mainstream culture has for the relationship roles of men and women and the ideals of masculinity and femininity. There are so many ways we might not fit in and then learn not to trust ourselves, relationships, and love. In reaction, it is easy to give up and despair, to blame ourselves for being inadequate, to isolate with the hope of gaining some protection through hiding, or to become actively cynical and negative, protecting oneself from getting drawn into trying to make a positive difference. Sometimes we become actively destructive in response, believing it's better to be actively negative than to feel weak and vulnerable. When we face long-term oppression of any kind, such responses are very human and common.

Once oppressed, it takes time to learn how to trust again, more time to risk loving again, and then even more time to trust feeling loveable and loved. Usually that learning has to occur within positive relationships, which are not necessarily easy to find in the midst of ongoing oppression. Despite progress, the oppression of misogyny, racism, economic oppression, and war continue.

As both Susan and the woman caught in adultery learned through their new relational experiences with Jesus and in psychotherapy, no one positive relationship takes away one's vulnerability. No human relationship can make us totally safe. However, one sustained positive relationship can make a significant difference toward hoping and then loving in the midst of our ongoing human vulnerability, even in the midst of ongoing oppression and danger.

What can happen over time in our relationships with Love, in our prayer with Love, is that we can learn to trust that Love is continually reaching out to us and in continual positive relationship with us, whether we are aware of the relationship or not, feel it or not, take it for granted or not. Learning to trust Love in this way most often begins with positive interactions with nature and people that over time can be seen to be reliable and repetitive.

It helps when these new experiences can be grounded upon our past or continual experiences with some combination of loving parents, family, and friends. But even when this ground is not available, we can become aware that the roots our new relationships are putting out can anchor us and be reinforced by our daily experiences of our world providing for us and then offering us special moments of beauty and awe. There is so much in our world that sustains us, that inspires us to keep growing, and for which we can be grateful.

As we attune ourselves to Love always working for us, loving us, it would not be surprising if we felt consoled and moved by gratefulness to contribute to Love's ongoing work in the world by loving more. Many of us will be moved to love where there is ongoing oppression and suffering, to help Love be more present and effective.

IMAGINE AND PONDER

- Once traumatized or while oppressed, it takes time to learn how to trust again, even more time to risk loving again, and then more time to trust feeling loveable and loved.

CHAPTER 14

OUR PAINFUL LIMITATIONS

(The Rich Young Man and The Apostles in the Garden)

These stories reflect our long-term suffering as we face our human limitations, what we call our weaknesses. What makes our limitations a source of suffering is that we often can do little to ameliorate them, and there is harsh self-judgment, regret, and most often shame attached to them. We usually feel shame when we don't live up to our best selves or our idealized selves, when we do not live up to our own good judgment or the judgement of others whose esteem we desire. Shame is often made worse when what we regret was witnessed, was done in public, or became known to others. Some degree of painful self-criticism and even self-punishment is also often present.

Regret and shame are perhaps the most common difficult feelings humans experience because they never need to end. None of us can change the past, so we cannot just make the reason for those feelings disappear. Nevertheless, we try to find ways to mitigate our regret and shame. We tend to want to hide with shame, sometimes we take our whole selves and run away. Mostly we tend to hide, isolate, or exile large parts of ourselves, compartmentalize them, and even lead dual lives. Those of us who can't just push away or hide our self-knowledge find it very difficult to accept that we have to live seemingly weak and flawed. The following transformed stories are meant to help us pray with our limitations and the sometimes intensely uncomfortable feelings that come with them.

THE RICH YOUNG MAN
(Mark 10:17-23; see also Matthew 19:16-22 and Luke 18:18-23)

A man ran up and knelt before Jesus, asking what he must do to inherit eternal life. Jesus reminded him of the biblical commandments. The man replied he had observed them since his youth. Jesus looked at him, loved him, and said, "You are lacking one thing. Go, sell what you have, give to the poor … then come, follow me." The man went away sad because he had many possessions.

THE TRANSFORMED STORY
(What happens later?)

Imagine the young man going away sad, sorely disappointed that he was not immediately awarded by Jesus. All he received was a look of love and a request for freer and more relationship. In addition, he also feels deep shame. He is not as perfect a fit for eternal life as he imagined. He regrets that he was so public in his confidence, because his shame is also so public. It was witnessed by many who know him or his reputation. What now can he do about his reputation? How can he show his face amidst those people who will see his limitation and judge him for it? How will he himself be able to accept his limitation?

He spends the rest of the day by himself, avoiding others, even those he knows care deeply about him. He is licking his wounds. That night, he sleeps poorly and awakes remembering that Jesus looked at him with love even as he admitted that he could not sell his possessions. He begins to feel Jesus's love even in the midst of his intense shame. There is no rejection or judgment of his whole person with that love. In fact, he gradually is sensing that Jesus continues to love and accept him, including his limitation.

He knows Jesus and his followers have not left the area, so the next morning he seeks out Jesus again. This time he is not bringing his achievements, perfection, or status. He will share his humanness, his awareness of his limitations, and his feelings about those limitations. He will share that he tentatively feels loved.

Curiously, while feeling loved, he knows that he is still attached to his riches. He knows and is not proud of that fact. Yet, he senses he is loved as a whole—attachments, ambition, and all the rest. This is the beginning of the young man's prayer and real relationship with Jesus in the midst of very human limitations.

A SECOND GOSPEL STORY: THE AGONY IN THE GARDEN

(Matthew 26:38–46)

After a period of prayer, Jesus found Peter, James, and John asleep. "So you could not keep watch with me for one hour?" He withdrew again to pray. When he returned the second time, he found them asleep again. He withdrew and prayed a third time. Upon returning, he said, "Are you still sleeping? . . . Get up, let us go. Look, my betrayer is at hand."

THE SECOND TRANSFORMED STORY
(What happens later?)

Imagine Peter, James, and John feel Jesus's disappointment, frustration, and anger at their not being able to stay awake nearby to pray with him. Even to them it does not seem a difficult request. They love him. They want to live up to his best visions of them, and their own best visions of themselves. They are ashamed that they couldn't.

Also, they remain competitive with each other for his esteem, and each of them fell short of his own expectations within the others' sight. That, too, feels shameful.

On this night in the Garden of Gethsemane, all this occurs without any time to personally talk it over with Jesus. He is arrested. They might not see him alive again, let alone have a chance to talk with him again. Their regret is intense. It may last as long as they live.

PRAYING WITH SHAME

Shame is such a prevalent and intense feeling for us humans. When any of us feel it, we often suffer with it, and it very often makes us hide from others, even ourselves, and isolates us.

Most of us humans feel it at some point in our lives in relationship to our bodies. We don't like to admit to or see, and especially have others see, the limitations of our bodies, natural ones that we are born with, ones that we contribute to through our diets or exercise, or ones that we take on through life—for example, through aging, illness, or other sources of damage.

Shame is also common among men because our culture continues to have a distorted ideal of men as not vulnerable, with no limitations, and with no weaknesses.

Shame cannot help coming into an intimate relationship. We don't always live up to our best selves, and an intimate relationship is a witness. However, a loving relationship can metabolize shame, take it in and use it to deepen the shared love.

In my years as a psychotherapist and psychoanalyst, I am sure I worked with over a thousand people. I myself was in psychoanalysis for many years, and over the course of my life worked with five psychotherapists. Through all of my experiences with others and with my own therapists, I learned it takes great courage and strength to come into deep relationship, even one that is purposefully structured to be safe and healing. That is because every psychotherapy begins with the courage and strength it takes to bring one's limitations out into the open and risk feeling the shame that is inevitable with asking for help. I know.

Of course, the same would be true of relating with Love in prayer. Any prayer with suffering involves courage and strength to face and share limitations and shame.

What helps in both therapy and prayer is to see the person you want help from waiting to welcome you with true understanding, not judgment, and most importantly with love, wanting to hear about and be affected by your experience and feelings. In therapy, because therapists are humans also, there are no guarantees you will find a therapist like that. You will have to test out gradually whether the therapist you are working with fits those very human needs of yours.

Similarly in prayer, we are still human and vulnerable. Especially when suffering, we will not immediately or totally trust Jesus or Love. We will start slowly, test whether we are met lovingly, and only trust gradually. Relationships develop over time. Beginning to pray with suffering is a risk, and one you can test out gradually. We answer Love's call to relationship with hope, not certainty.

In the transformed story of the rich young man, the man realizes that Jesus didn't reject him due to his limitations. Jesus didn't stop loving him. The man went away out of shame. Jesus didn't go anywhere. The man had to test that out. He had to return and see how he was treated. Probably more than once. Probably he tested the depth of Jesus's love over time. That is only human, the way a human deepens relationship. Hopefully he continued to experience how Jesus welcomed him back, repeatedly, to share himself and his whole story, limitations, shame, and all the rest.

In the transformed story of the sleepy apostles, it is easy to imagine that as the events of Jesus's passion unfolded, and in the years afterward, whenever these men remembered disappointing Jesus and themselves, they suffered. They probably continued to have high expectations for themselves as friends of Jesus. Hopefully they learned to accept their limitations and their humanness, even knowing that they would disappoint Jesus again and again.

Fortunately, the apostles had a shared history of a few years of showing Jesus their limitations and experiencing Jesus's continuing love for them. Maybe they were able to see or at least feel Jesus's love for them as he led the way to his arrest, as he was taken from them. Hopefully, they learned, in a way that remained in their hearts, that he would continue to look at them with love, welcome them into his presence, and be interested in all they had to share around their experiences and feelings of love for him—their expectations, his expectations, and their continuing limitations. I imagine this was often how their conscious prayer would begin in the coming years: Jesus looking at them with Love and desiring more relationship. And just maybe they fell asleep less often in the midst of their prayer.

IMAGINE AND PONDER

- We want both to be truly known by a loving other and to avoid being known in particular ways. We have mixed motivations. Love knows about the mixed motivations of humans and loves us with our limitations and vulnerabilities, our weaknesses. Once loved in this way, we feel freer and feel most grateful for this gift.

CHAPTER 15

OUR DAMAGED HOME

(Jesus Curses a Fig Tree)

This chapter is for those who suffer with the earth, our home, and in specific environments. It is also for all of us who painfully contribute to the earth's degradation.

JESUS CURSES A FIG TREE
(Mark 11:12-14 and 20-21; see also Matthew 21:18-22 and Luke 13:6-9)

Jesus and his followers were walking. He was hungry. When he saw a fig tree, he went to see if it had any figs even though it wasn't the season for figs. It had no figs. He cursed the tree, "May no one ever eat of your fruit again!" The next day they were walking by the same tree and they all noticed it was withered to its roots.

THE TRANSFORMED STORY
(What happens later?)

Imagine that yesterday we were able to greet Jesus as he and his people passed through our neighborhood. What we witnessed shocked us. It was so different from what we expected. We heard him curse a fig tree for not having figs ... *out of season*! It withered overnight.

Now this morning as Jesus returns, we yell, "Whoa! Jesus! Stop! Wait!" He does stop. He is looking at us. Coming up close to him, it is difficult to read his face. Is he impatient? Angry? His people are agitated, and he may be too. Maybe his mind and heart are elsewhere, on Jerusalem. It is not easy to confront him. Yet, I do. "Jesus, I have heard you speak, appreciating the seasons, our natural world, and the land many of us tend that generously gives us its bounty. What are you doing damaging a life-giving tree? A gift of your Father and mine? It is a gift that helps feed us and shade us, and you destroy it! How self-centered you are in this act! How harmful! If you want to make a point, do you have to make it by harming an innocent living creature? If you have poisonous feelings, like all of us, there have to be better ways to deal with them. Will you return life to this tree you killed?"

Jesus is taking longer breaths now. Gradually, I also see him taking in more about me and my little group. We are feeling tentative all of sudden, a bit shaky, given my surprising indignation, and a bit fearful after I called him out on his destructive behavior. I wonder if Job felt all this as he confronted God about God's destructiveness in his life.

Slowly Jesus's whole body seems to soften. He looks at us with a dignity that comes with self-possession. He seems to be recognizing and acknowledging our dignity. Gradually, his sorrow and empathy for the earth, himself, and us are also coming through to us.

This is the beginning of prayer, of conscious relationship with Love and our earthly home.

A CONTEMPORARY TRANSFORMATION

Love is waiting for us.

Love will not be surprised by confrontation.

Love knows as we do that there has been birth and death from the beginning of time. After all, the universe began with a big explosion. Matter and its elements have been forming, breaking apart, and reforming. Stars and everything else have been birthed and have died, formed, changed, and reformed in extraordinary combinations. In the midst of this evolution, whole species of organisms on earth have come and gone. Love knows loss.

Love is not surprised by our direct confrontation: Why does death and destruction have to follow birth and creativity? Why so much loss?

Of course, Love can also see that as we use our gifts of consciousness and free will, we often are actively contributing to death and loss. Love knows our common home, our most valuable and shared responsibility as humans, is suffering at our own hands. At an accelerating rate, habitats are being actively destroyed, animals and plants are actively being extinguished, and so many of the earth's peoples, who are trying to justly live in the simplest ways, are painfully being flooded out of their homelands or having to emigrate because of heat and drought. We also confront each other with these facts.

Love is waiting for us. What else can we say to express ourselves and enter into deeper relationship? What can we do?

This is only one possibility:

> Love, it seems you must know the sorrow of massive loss as well as the joys of awesome creativity and beauty. Through your empathy for us and Jesus's own decisions, you know

> what it is like to be human with so many mixed motivations and mixed results. You must also know that we often harm the things and people we love. We face so much grief, hold so much guilt. Still, we love this world and all its life. We desire it all to flourish.
>
> Is hope possible? Are we just witnessing and participating in the endless, repetitive birth-and-death nature of existence, or is it leading somewhere? Is it leading only to more death? Given our conscious capacities for choosing and developing love, is positive evolution still possible?
>
> How then might we respond to those suffering now and those in imminent danger on our earth? How might we respond to the earth we love and are responsible for, even as we damage it?
>
> We are grateful you continue to love us, but it certainly seems we need more help if we are not to increase suffering and eventually extinguish life on earth as we know it.
>
> Does each fig tree matter? Does each of us humans matter? Should we care?
>
> Love, help us discern and attune ourselves to you and what we love. Help our love make a positive difference.

This is a version of my frequent prayer with Love for our vulnerable, beautiful, life-sustaining home.

CONFRONTING IN PRAYER

As I wrote this chapter, it became clear to me why this book was difficult to write and difficult to read. It not only calls forth your and my experiences of chronic suffering; it also is filled with confrontation. Confronting someone you love is difficult. Confronting someone you would like to love if you could only trust them more is also difficult.

More explicitly in this chapter than in others, Jesus, considered by many the face of Love, chooses to do something that is not loving but damaging, albeit limited, and you might even say murderous. And we confront him. I call that prayer, the conscious participation in what could be an ongoing deepening loving relationship.

All of the confrontations in this book include anger. They may not feel loving. Yet, they are. When people contribute to our suffering, it would be only natural to harshly judge them, then stay far away, reject them, and not even acknowledge their existence. Suffering stresses trust, sometimes to the breaking point.

However, our confrontations in prayer are loving because they involve an intimate sharing of what hurts and why. Judgment is not final. The person confronting remains open and watchful for responses that suggest recognition, empathy, sorrow, and care. If your story is heard and felt, has an effect, without leading to retaliation, and it only leads to circumscribed defensiveness, then you might feel known and safe. All of those responses are signs that you, including your confronting story, are valued. They are signs of desire and care for relationship. If those signs are repeated, they build trust. As sharing continues, intimacy and love may develop.

Long-term serious wounds like we share in this book have to be opened, or, in many cases, reopened, if they are not to fester and become infected. They must be opened toward the healing fresh air and light of a developing intimate loving relationship. What can be healing is learning through experience that in fact Love bears all things, including anger, responsibility, and people who confront. Actually, in my experience, Love holds all things lovingly.

IMAGINE AND PONDER

- If your story is heard and felt, has an effect, without leading to dismissal or retaliation, then you might feel known and safe. These are signs you are valued. If those signs are repeated, they build trust. As sharing continues, intimacy and love may develop.

CHAPTER 16

GROUP CHOICES: HOPE FALLS TOWARD DESPAIR

(The Crowd Chooses Barabbas over Jesus)

This chapter is for those remaining very disappointed, sad, and fearful for months or years after a series of group choices or votes in which your neighbors, friends, family members, or fellow citizens chose differently than you. Their choices reflect that their most basic understanding of the situation or most basic values are opposed to yours with no apparent room for compromise or meeting around shared interests. As a result, you see and fear significant suffering coming for innocent others and those trying to do good. The suffering could be coming to you, too, and even to those who chose differently than you. Choices like these are the moments the floor falls from beneath us, and we are full of dread. Hope free falls toward despair. Large underground fissures break the surface in our families or community or across our society, even within other nations, and widen dangerously. We cry out in prayer in this fragile time, in the midst of fear of long-term unending suffering. We are in the midst of such strong human tendencies to double down on our limited perspectives, to take advantage of and scapegoat others, and to disassociate, to become numb, immune, and uncaring.

THE CROWD CHOOSES BARABBAS
(Luke 23:13-25, as well as Mark 15:6-15, John 18:28 to 19:16, and Matthew 27:15-26)

The high priests determined that Jesus was guilty and should be put death. They went with their guards and Jesus to the praetorium so Pilate would judge Jesus. Three times Pilate brought Jesus out before the high priests and some of the public. Three times they wanted Barabbas (a rebel and murderer) freed instead of Jesus. They repeatedly said they wanted Jesus crucified, not just scourged.

THE TRANSFORMED GOSPEL STORY
(What happens next?)

Imagine we find ourselves in the crowd outside the praetorium after Jesus is condemned. You find yourself crying out loudly to him from your tortured spirit, "We could have saved you, Jesus! You and all your work! Why didn't we save you? Three times we had the chance! Look at us!" And he is looking at each of us, the crowd's individuals, those devastated by what has just happened, those who are jumping and shouting jubilantly, those spewing hate. Jesus was looking the entire time, at each of us, each time we voted with our voices. He is unbowed and yet weeping, looking at whoever will meet his gaze. Looking with compassion and love.

Others in this crowd were also touched by Jesus. They are terrified for him and for what his execution will mean for all those who have felt hope over the last three years. Something was changing within all of us that made us see and treat ourselves and each other differently, with more respect, care, and generosity, in ways that demonstrated we are in this life together, interrelated, and that we all belong. He acted in service of everyone. He practiced mercy to all.

But he didn't touch everyone, or not with the same power, and some are angry about that, envious or jealous. Some are fearful of the changes he was bringing, some reject him as dangerous to the status quo that many adapted to, and some are simply misinformed, misguided by forces beyond them.

The world that held us all is being turned upside down and shaken. What will happen to us?

We cry out! To him, for him, for us, our neighbors, our world.

This is the most natural prayer: assuming relationship and love, and crying out.

A CONTEMPORARY TRANSFORMATION

It seems Love isn't always a clear choice, and there are many obstacles to choosing a more intimate relationship with Love.

Laura and Joe are a middle-aged couple, both with jobs, and they are parents to four young children. Laura's elderly and infirm father, Ed, lives far away and can no longer take care of himself physically. He also can no longer take care of or afford his own home. Ed has three sisters who live near him. They visit him, but they do not contribute to his care physically or financially, let alone the upkeep of his house. They are adamant that their brother should not be placed in a nursing home. His daughter, Laura, feels like she has no choice but to have her father cared for in a nursing home. Laura's aunts threaten that if she places her father there, they will not visit him again or talk with Laura. Laura pleads with them to understand her own personally painful situation regarding the choices she has to care for her father and asks for their physical and financial help. They refuse.

Laura and Joe are friends of mine I have known for years. It turns out Laura chose to place her father in a quality home, near where he lived all his adult life, where he was well cared for the rest of his life. Her aunts chose to stick with their threats. They never visited their brother, never talked again with Laura, and didn't go to their brother's funeral and burial. The family as a whole was devastated. Laura lost family, cousins, and aunts she grew up with and was attached to. Her children lost the opportunity to have a greater extended family. Her sadness is poignant even now, years later. So is her anger. I don't think Laura is very religious. However, when it was all happening, I am sure Laura cried out to her aunts for love's sake. I'm sure she cried out loud into the universe for help as she and her aunts faced the choices that led to their extended family's destruction. I doubt Laura thought she was praying when she cried out in these ways. If she thought about it, she may have felt angry at a God who didn't seem actively on the side of love. Love seemed to be diminishing in her family, not increasing; weakening, not coming together to flourish around her father's gradual dying. I understand her crying out was prayer, whether to her aunts for love or into the universe to Love. She was crying to be known and understood as a loving daughter and mother, a woman oriented to family, crying out for help. I know Laura felt she was choosing to love her father the best ways she could. I cannot speak for her aunts. Maybe they, too, thought they were crying out for love when they threatened Laura. I don't know.

But as I write this, I am struck by the fact that in this case I know more about Love. I know Laura is grateful for her husband Joe's ongoing love for her and how he experiences her as a loving woman. I know she appreciates Joe's compassion for what she experienced in her relationship with her elderly father. I know my and others' love for our friend Laura is not insignificant to her, and she also appreciates our compassion for what she experienced while actively loving her father. And, in noting all this, I know I once again am not able to separate love from Love.

CONSCIOUS PRAYER

Prayer is relationship with Love. Relationships don't have to be verbalized, and they don't have to be conscious. We are relating to everything around us all the time through our actions and with our feelings, and we are not aware of most of those interactions. We cannot help but be in relationship with Love because Love loves us first and continually through our relationships with all things. Love is always gazing upon us with a wholeness that sees our values, limitations and intentions, feelings and actions, all our diverse parts and our attempts at integrating them. However, Love also desires to know us more and desires more for us. For example, wouldn't Love appreciate hearing, in our own words, our own perspectives on ourselves and our lives. Even more so, wouldn't Love desire us to have more love and life in our lives, to flourish, by working intimately with us in loving others and our world.

IMAGINE AND PONDER

- When Love is not publicly chosen and even scourged, the love in our personal lives is essential. We need it to sustain ourselves. Gradually it will fuel our efforts to attune ourselves again to the work of Love on a broader scale so that Love may flourish in our communities and the world.

CHAPTER 17

JESUS AND HIS FELLOW REVOLUTIONARIES

(Jesus on the Cross)

These stories are for those of us who devote major parts of our lives to making the world a more just and humane place. Suffering comes from the sometimes overwhelming forces working against us and Love. We often cannot help ourselves from being angry at Jesus or Love, at times for not doing more for justice, love, and life.

JESUS ON THE CROSS
(Matthew 27:38-44 and then Luke 23:39-43)

Two revolutionaries were crucified with Jesus. Many who were watching, including the people's leaders, reviled him. The two revolutionaries abused him too. One yelled, "Are you not the Messiah? Save yourself and us." The other responded, "Have you no fear of God?" The sentences we received correspond to our crimes, but this man has done nothing criminal." He then said to Jesus, "Remember me when you come into your kingdom." Jesus said, "Today you will be with me in Paradise."

THE TRANSFORMED STORY
(What else is happening?)

Three people following different paths end up suffering together. Isn't this the way it always is? Different ways to get to where and when the earth quakes or a trainwreck happens, to the front lines of an attack in war, to where the missile hits, the bomb goes off, or the mass murderer walks in. These three were each a revolutionary in his own way in a brutally occupied land. Though they didn't know each other, they knew they held this in common. They also experienced the same source of excruciating physical pain and suffering.

So they have significant things in common, yet each suffering person comes with different struggles and a different history. Imagine that both of the men being crucified with Jesus have heard of him and his reputation for healing and bringing people back from the dead. The people watching have heard the same stories. Some might have witnessed those astounding happenings.

Of course people yell for him to save himself and his fellows! Of course the two men next to him cry out too! Most witnesses to this suffering want it to end quickly, pray for it to end. Didn't we hear Jesus himself cry, "My God, my God, why have you forsaken me?" Maybe he can't bear it all. Maybe he tried to save them all from this torture, . . . but he couldn't. Maybe he couldn't access his power to save or heal under such intensely personal and painful pressure.

And there are other reasons for these two men to pressure Jesus any way they can. Wouldn't his saving them be a terrorizing blow to those occupiers and religious leaders who condemned them? Could this torture be worthwhile if it ended that way? If either man hopes that Jesus actually has the power they have heard about, wouldn't he plead with him to use it and be angry if he didn't?

It also would not be surprising at all if any hope they had eventually turned to jeering and rebuke. They must protect themselves from the vulnerability of hope, how can they be so foolish as to hope? How can they let themselves feel there is any way out? Fueled by disappointment, hope only makes the suffering worse and leads down the path to despair. Don't they have to taunt him to hold aggressively onto the meaning of their lives, to the idea that fighting for freedom is worthwhile no matter the cost? Doesn't he also fight for that?

Imagine, too, that when he is not caught up in his own bodily suffering or naturally is dissociating from it, they can see him listening to them, slowly turning his aching head from one to the other, looking at them when he can, meeting their eyes, and his eyes are filled with compassion. He understands and feels the power of their rebukes and all their varied feelings stored up, now spewing from inside them. There is no way he can be angry at them, let alone condemn them. He knows them.

He knows they used different methods to reach their goals. He used love. They were more indiscriminate, ruthless. His vision of freedom was more expansive and grounded differently, in love, which was always implicated in everything he did. Still, he listens and holds their feelings and gazes. For a while the three of them are contained in their own shared bubble of pain. The people nearby, those on the ground, those not immersed in being crucified, seem far away, not even present. These two men with Jesus see his compassion for them, how he feels for them in their suffering, while he also suffers. In response, one yells at the other to stop rebuking Jesus, and then asks something of Jesus. Jesus clearly comforts him, somehow, even in the midst of their pain.

The other man doesn't stop. Jesus listens and then again looks at him with a love the man feels. He continues to rail against Jesus's inadequacy, the injustices they are victims of, the darkness blanketing their world, and, yes, the darkness that this man knows he contributed to and feels terrible about. It is all prayer. He has made a connection with Jesus. They are in relationship as they die together.

A CONTEMPORARY TRANSFORMATION

In a group I meet with periodically, there is a professor who teaches business ethics, an emergency room physician, a special education teacher, and a public defender—one who works with death row capital punishment cases. They are my peers, my neighbors, and my friends. They grew up in religious households of one kind or another, have given up much of their religious beliefs, and participate little in those institutions. Each one could list the sources of their frustration and anger at the established order of values and power in our society. Quite admirably, they have each found their own way to do good, to contribute to a better world. Each could talk movingly of the people they work with and for whom they care deeply. Each is empathically suffering with and for our society and the people in it. Yes, part of their suffering is that they know they are not innocent. We all contribute at least indirectly to the systems, the principalities and powers, that desecrate our common earthly home, oppress others by limiting their opportunities, and judge without mercy.

Of course, Love would be interested in these people trying to do good even in the midst of their limitations and inadequacies, their frustrations and anger. Love would see their suffering. I imagine Love waiting and wanting to hear from each of my friends.

So, picture with me that one of my friends portrayed here feels the opportunity, realizes she has been searching for it, and approaches Love. She has no trouble approaching. In fact, as she approaches and feels something of Love's gaze, she feels stronger in her convictions and more emboldened to speak. Seizing the moment, she expresses her anger, variations on, "Where have you been? Where are you now with these people I care about? What are you doing now to help?" Her anger blazes into rage. Intense. Blinding. It's been stored up for so long, it is flooding out. She loses track of Love's gaze, the sense of Love's presence.

As the flood recedes, she can feel it will just be for the moment. It will return, like the incoming waves of the tide in a storm. The tide will return, as will the storms. She knows the people she works for and with, those on her side and those in opposition, and she will be returning to them when she finishes speaking with Love.

In this brief quiet, she gives voice as well to her guilt, regrets, and inadequacies. She again is beginning to feel that Love is listening, wanting to hear it all, to know her, with mercy and compassion.

As she does this, she is responding within her relationship with Love and consciously praying. As she returns to her everyday life, trying to bring more justice and love into the world, she will gradually, consciously bring this relationship with Love along with her, attuning herself to Love.

REPETITION IN PRAYER, THE CONSTANCY OF SUFFERING AND LOVE

With ongoing suffering, prayer will always be repetitive. It can't be any other way. The sources of ongoing suffering usually do not go away. Typically, if they do go away, it is only partially, only gradually, and there is always the possibility of a return. And then there are the memories of suffering that sometimes can last a lifetime.

In any given moment, severe suffering can overwhelm our capacities to receive love and to give it. Given those facts, it is very important to note that often severe suffering makes it impossible to even think about prayer or Love. Hopefully in those moments others will pray for us and, even more importantly, actively lovingly care for us.

The transformed stories in this chapter highlight what can be a painful struggle over a lifetime to make a difference in others' suffering. We struggle to love more and better while there remains so much in our society working against our efforts and so many natural limitations within ourselves. Usually, our relationships with suffering are long-term.

No wonder it is difficult to believe in God.

However, this brings us to one of the useful and clarifying aspects of addressing God as Love or in some other personal way. Simultaneously with suffering, many of us have numerous long-term love relationships, perhaps with the natural world, one or more friends, partners, children, and pets. Loving relationships, relationships with Love, are also fairly constant and available throughout life. Often, they are sources of consolation in the midst of suffering.

Love does not intend us to suffer. While Love may not protect us from suffering or make suffering disappear, Love doesn't abandon us. Most accurately, Love is with us in our suffering—consoling us, affirming us, perhaps gradually strengthening us for some active response to what we suffer. This active response might be eating a bit of food in a weakened condition, trying to smile at one of our caregivers, taking medication, getting out of bed, standing up to a bully, voting, volunteering, or calling a friend.

Love, then, is not typically a tool to get rid of suffering. Love is an ongoing relationship that often helps decenter and metabolize the suffering that is a part of our lives. Since Love is a relationship, of course we will share with Love how we are doing, what we feel, what we desire, on an ongoing basis—perhaps daily or more often. Of course we will complain and confront, especially if we feel our suffering is taking over the rest of our life. Good relationships often can handle that kind of honesty, that kind of love. Love wants to know and be known. Knowing our suffering is part of being known. Hoping and trying to flourish in the midst of suffering, Love is with us. Loving each other as we express our suffering is part of participating with Love.

IMAGINE AND PONDER

- Listening to each other, even repetitively, as we express our suffering is part of Love loving us.

CHAPTER 18

DESPAIR AND DESCENT

(Why Have You Forsaken Me? and Descent into Hell)

The following transformed Gospel story follows naturally from all the previous ones in this book. Yet it may not be for everyone. If prayer cries out to Love, and we know that in the Gospels Jesus prays, to whom does Jesus cry out when he comes face to face with others' suffering? To whom does Jesus cry out when he himself suffers? To whom does Jesus express his human anger? With whom does Jesus want to share all this? In the Gospels he addresses his cries, his prayer, to his Father. Some readers may not want to think of Jesus sharing suffering with his Father, let alone his anger. Others will quickly feel that of course he did!

You may have heard someone say they love God, and, still, when they get to heaven they intend to ask God some pointed questions about God's role in suffering—if not intending it, what about allowing it? The following transformed Gospel story imagines Jesus after his death sharing his fully human challenging feelings and experiences with his Father, within Love, and Love's responses to that sharing.

I offer these stories as an affirmation for crying out to Love with your full human experience. If we can share our experience of human suffering with Jesus, and Jesus responds compassionately, then we can imagine Jesus sharing his human suffering with his Father, and his Father opening to it, responding compassionately, being Love.

MY GOD, MY GOD, WHY HAVE YOU FORSAKEN ME?

(Matthew 27:45-47 and Mark 15:33-34)

Jesus is crucified. He cries out, "My God, my God, why have you forsaken me?" These are some of his last words before giving up his spirit and dying. Tradition says that he is quoting Psalm 22:2, expressing despair and anger in the face of a torturous death. Tradition also has it, explicitly in the Apostles' Creed and somewhat supported by a number of scripture passages, that after dying Jesus descended into hell.

THE TRANSFORMED STORY

(What happens later?)

Imagine we are there, painfully and helplessly witnessing Jesus's torturous death. Suddenly, we hear him cry out, "My God, my God, why have you forsaken me?" We are also there as he dies. Now imagine with me, and I know this is asking a lot, that we are there when he enters heaven. Son and Father fall into each other's joyous arms. Though it was done willingly, they have been separated, or more differentiated from each other, for thirty-three human years. That time must feel way too long to them. Love flows between them. That loving Spirit is alive and well.

Yet there is something else now present, something new between them, the personal experience of being human, of suffering as humans do, and having the additional personal human experiences of witnessing those you identify with and love suffer as well. Jesus holds all this in his human body and memories. What of all this does Jesus convey to his Father? What are the effects? I imagine they are profoundly upsetting to both. I imagine both search each other's eyes amidst their tears for acceptance and understanding. I picture natural human anger expressed and some pointed questions: "How could you, Father, be involved in all the suffering I witnessed? How could you be involved in the suffering I went through myself? How could we, Love, be a part of all the suffering of creation and evolution?" I picture this confrontation with suffering as disturbing. I imagine "it feels like hell," perhaps like Love descending into hell. That may be a feeling and realization valuable to sit with a while.

Still, the story doesn't end there. Compassionately, Love makes room for the experiences of human suffering and the suffering in creation. Then, even in what feels like hell, that compassionate response creates the possibility of life and love rising again. It may be similar to the advent of germinating seeds in darkness under harsh conditions.

A CONTEMPORARY TRANSFORMATION

Obviously, we have no way of knowing for sure what happened in the couple days after Jesus died. If there was a dialogue or conversation of any sort, it was a dialogue *within Love*. Through scripture and tradition, we do know that Jesus was human and expressed to his Father acute fear and feelings of despair and anger during his passion. I just pictured, after Jesus died, the back-and-forth between him and his Father, within Love, trying to integrate ongoing painful human experience and the suffering of creation into the whole of Love and into Love's ongoing love relationships.

Here is a contemporary very human story that I pray with every day. It, too, tries to integrate challenging ongoing painful human experiences within loving relationships and in relationship with Love.

My mother, who has been in hospice for almost a year, is very gradually, slowly dwindling under the watchful eyes of all those who care about her. She complained recently about how difficult everything is for her. I was holding her hand, and said as carefully as I could, wanting to help her with part of the truth of her situation, "Well, you know, mom, I think you're coming to the end." Immediately she responded, "Yeah, I don't know how to get there." Hearing that, my heart broke open. So many times she cries aloud at night and pleads, "I want to go home," and she is in the home she has lived in for over fifty years. Often, I tell her that all of us who are with her, love her and are trying to companion her to get there. And yet, we cannot just take her home. There is no clear route and no shortcut. In addition to its being long and slow, this is a meandering journey that we are accompanying her on. One caregiver said it is between her and God now. We have no idea when she will turn some familiar-looking corner and we'll all be surprised that she's finally arrived.

Recently one of my brothers and I shared memories of very positive times we had with our mother while we were growing up and she was focused on making our lives happy. We were sad that we couldn't actively share those memories with our mother now. She couldn't connect to them and they wouldn't bring her happiness, just confusion or frustration. I was also sad that my mother has changed. She is still the same person, but her access to the ways she used to be engaged in the world are not available to her now. Her humor, her intelligence, her practicality, even her empathy, are all greatly limited. When I tell people about my mother now at ninety-eight, or when people meet her, they all say they are impressed with her strength, her overall health, and her determination. Almost all of these good people also say they would not want to be living like she does now. I understand. There are days it can seem like hell.

I imagined Jesus and his Father had to integrate direct human experience into their loving relationship, into Love. I have to try to come to terms with and integrate into the whole loving relationship I have had and held with my mother over seventy years, the difficult and painful experiences of the last few years, and this last year especially. Sometimes it is difficult and sad not to clearly see the mother I knew within the mother I now relate to and still love. Not surprisingly, I pray about this all with Love every day. I let Love know my sadness around missing the mother I knew. I let Love know how desperately I feel for Love to guide her home safely and quickly so she doesn't suffer more as she is. Sometimes that desperation comes with frustration and anger. I cry out to Love for my mother. I ask for help loving her and the people who care for her 24/7. I want to be a good shepherd to all of them. Those caregivers need support. I pray that their wells of patience, perseverance, and love don't go dry. I pray, trusting that Love is active and not asleep, not powerless, to shepherd us all as we try our best to love my mother home.

WHOLENESS

I know about human trauma. I know that it has to find some release, some expression, and some place in the whole of our experience. What I imagined in the relationship between Jesus and his Father, what I pray about in my relationship with my mother, is consistent with human experience and my experience with Love; suffering needs some physical and emotional release, some expression and some compassionate meeting. I know love is often not easy, wholeness can be painful, still Love has room and compassion for all people and all experience, darkness and light, anger and gratitude, despair and hope. Every story in this book is like a seed planted amidst harsh conditions in this loving ground of our being. Love desires with active compassion the germination of those seeds in the dark and our communal flourishing.

I am reminded of the classic children's book, *The Velveteen Rabbit.* The book portrays toys becoming real through love. There are parallels to how I picture us humans called by Love to wholeness. At one point, the toys are conversing about how they are vulnerable as they are loved and become real. They ask the wise old rocking horse, "Does it hurt to become real?" The rocking horse answers, "The more real you become, the less you mind that it hurts."

IMAGINE AND PONDER

- Love knows suffering and is changed by suffering.

Love takes suffering into itself so that what suffers, even Love, can eventually be transformed and bring new life.

CHAPTER 19

THE REMAINS OF SUFFERING: TRAUMA

(A Post-Resurrection Story)

This chapter is for people whose acute suffering is over, or, probably more accurately, in some way it is in the near or distant past. It may be in the past, but it is not forgotten. The memory of it is painful and maybe frightening as well. The scars, the associations that bring it to mind, and the consequences continue to negatively affect the present. That's post-traumatic stress.

This chapter also illustrates that when one person traumatically suffers, others suffer through association. When a lethal shooter enters a school, for example, children and teachers who are not physically harmed often suffer traumatically. We humans are naturally inextricably interconnected. We have evolved to be capable of loving interconnection. That's us at our best, and it's what the world needs. If we can't protect each other, we try to heal and console. Yet the interconnections of love make us more vulnerable, not less. Loving someone who is traumatically suffering can bring traumatic suffering to us.

APPEARANCES TO THE DISCIPLES
(John 20:19-29)

Within days of Jesus's Crucifixion, his followers had locked themselves in a room in fear for their own lives. Jesus appeared to them, saying, "Peace be with you." When they told Thomas, who had not been there, about this, he said, "Unless I . . . put my finger into the nail marks and put my hand into his side, I will not believe."

Jesus's followers were still locked in the room a week later, but now Thomas was with them. Jesus entered the locked room and repeated, "Peace be with you." He told Thomas to probe his wounds and believe. Thomas did so and exclaimed, "My Lord and my God!"

THE TRANSFORMED STORY
(What else is happening?)

Imagine we are in the locked room with Mary Magdalene, Mary (Jesus's mother), eleven of his closest followers (including Thomas), and others. All of us have seen, or heard about someone seeing, the crucified and risen Jesus. While we all are feeling a bit of excitement and hope, we mostly feel intense waves of general anxiety, fear, and doubt. We are overwhelmed by the violence we witnessed, anxious about how dangerous and unsafe humans are. We are also fearful that what happened to him will happen to all of us. Our grief is still with us too. Our teacher and friend, Jesus, was tortured and crucified. He died and was buried. We cannot forget those facts. Some of us understandably break into tears as we sit, so full of tension, in this shared space.

It was a week ago when the transformed Jesus mysteriously appeared among many of us and said, "Peace." Yet, here we are a week later. Same locked room. Still traumatized. Same anxiety, fear, and doubt. Same sadness and mourning.

And, while there is some sense that everything has changed, and Jesus has changed, still, how can we be at peace? How can we not be afraid? Aren't we still dangerously vulnerable?

Thomas is among us this week. He has not seen or interacted with Jesus since before Jesus's death. Thomas has said aloud to all of us that he will not accept that Jesus has been raised from the dead until he sees and touches Jesus's wounds. His saying this helps clarify something for all of us. We all knew and loved Jesus through his love for and suffering with others. He loved each of us too. He knew and was compassionate toward each of us with our inadequacies and limitations. He was one of us. He saw how we tried to love and suffered, and we saw how he loved and suffered.

Of course it would be the case that Thomas would trust him again only if he could see Jesus's wounds, the physical signs of his suffering. We could not trust it was Jesus and that he was still one of us if we could not still see evidence of his suffering. Isn't that how it is with all of us? We cannot trust someone fully, even their love for us, if we do not know some of how they have suffered themselves and whether they could compassionately be with us in our suffering.

OH! Here Jesus is again. Standing in front of Thomas. What's happening?

I feel this room may burst with the intensity and confusion of all we feel in this moment. How can we even hear him speak? "Touch my wounds."

He is looking at each of us. He is saying, to each of us, "Come close, as close as you want. Touch my wounds. Recognize me as the one who has always loved you. I have always known your wounds and suffered with you. Come close and see my wounds; come close and touch."

We each feel and respond within the relationships we have had with him. We are consciously praying.

A CONTEMPORARY TRANSFORMATION

We know ourselves most intimately through knowing our bodies, our wounds (physical and emotional), our suffering, and who and what we have loved. Love desires to know us in these ways, and I daresay we desire to be known by Love in these ways. Our best and most intimate relationships are relationships where we are vulnerable and lovingly known, maybe especially with our suffering.

Recently, after retiring, I met with a woman, Belle. I had worked with her on and off from the beginning of my career. Her father had just died. Through a terrible last hospital stay in which the staff was neglectful, he suffered waves of excruciating pain. It wasn't until he finally was admitted to a hospice and was appropriately medicated that he calmed down and had significant relief. It was treatment he had been requesting, screaming for. Then he calmly died.

After not seeing Belle for months, we hugged hello, she handed me some baked goods, I thanked her, I lit a candle in honor of her and her dead parents, and she went right to work telling me how confused and upset she was. She was tearful all the while she described her own suffering as her father had suddenly been overcome by waves of pain, as she tried to assess what he needed, assuage his pain, communicate with her siblings, fight for her father's care with the hospital staff, and manage her own life responsibilities. She related how she also suddenly learned he was dying and needed hospice.

She knew I was there to listen to her, to her whole story, the last weeks before and immediately after her father died, including all her feelings, her fear, her active desperate love, her anger, her grief, her guilt, and the needed consolation she experienced with the hospice staff. She also told me about her prayer during her father's dying. She shared her doubts about her prayer and still how it was consoling at times. She said I was the only person so far who could hear it all. Ninety minutes after we began, we hugged again. She left calmer, more sure of herself, even within the continuing painful swirl of so many feelings and changes in her life.

Over the years, Belle, this loving, smart, oh-so-talented woman consistently let me know her in her suffering. Often it was suffering I could not do anything to take away. I offered perspective. I held it with her, at least for a brief time, and I witnessed to it. I know her in many ways, including her talents and joys, but one of the most profound is that I know her in her suffering.

PRAYER AND LOVE AS ATTUNEMENT AND WAYS OF BEING CHANGED

I feel the work I did in my career was loving *and* it was prayer. Truth be told, I feel that way about all my relationships. I feel I can say that because I try to attune myself to Love within those relationships, to answer Love's call in those relationships.

What does attuning and resonating with Love in relationships mean?

I learn about myself as I pray while in relationship with others. I never quite know what will be drawn out of me. Similarly, and most importantly, I am present to learn, listen, take in, be affected by whatever others share with me, in their actions and their words. As I attune myself to others and let myself be deeply affected by them, even changed by knowing them, I feel Love is helping me do for others what Love desires to do for them. Love desires to know and be with all of us in our pain and suffering. Love is empathically pained by it all and shares in it, as I do with the people I worked with over my career and continue to deeply care about. I want to be open to Love (and in the moment, that is conscious prayer), to be able to serve Love and the people I care about the way I do, getting to know them empathically and intimately. Love knows me as I actively care about and am affected by them.

IMAGINE AND PONDER

- We are vulnerable to trauma through the interconnections of love. As we recognize and let ourselves be deeply affected by others, including their trauma, we can be transformed and help do for others what Love desires to do for them.

PART 2

DEEPEN PRAYER'S ROOTS WITH AWARENESS, ATTUNEMENT, AND GRATITUDE

While continuing to express our suffering, the three ways we deepen our relationship with Love are these:

- Be **Aware**—There is always more going on in our lives than suffering. Attention to *the more* is crucial.
- **Attune**—In the midst of suffering, Love is coming our way, working for us, calling to us, and inviting our participation. Attuning to and participating with Love is also crucial.
- Be **Grateful**—Being thankful is the easiest way to deepen the positive effects of being loved, to let love soak into our cores, and to enjoy love. Even while suffering, appreciating the love coming our way is the easiest way to love in return. Being grateful naturally leads to passing love along to others with joy.

CHAPTER 20

THE FEELING EXPERIENCE OF PRAYER: AN ANALOGY CORRECTED

Many years ago, I attended a professional workshop that took place in a large hotel ballroom with sparkling chandeliers but no tables or chairs. There were one hundred participants. We were told to let out a loud sound of any kind on the count of three. We did, and it was hideous! A cacophony that was dissonant, irritating, and very loud. Many people held their hands over their ears. We were told to hold aloud our individual sounds, repeat them with each breath, walk around the ballroom until we met one or more people holding the same tone, and then raise our hands.

This is actually a task that requires an intense focus. Firstly, it is not easy holding onto and blaring out or singing what seems to be our own unique sound in the midst of a jungle of other noises. At first, the chaos becomes louder because each person is trying to hear and attend to their own note above the others. Then, as we begin our search for accurate resonance, we have to temper our volume in order to become more aware of the other notes we pass. We listen for a match. Though we have better odds, the search feels like the auditory equivalent of finding a needle in a haystack.

As I meandered through the crowd, within a minute or two, I could hear or see a few people, a couple at a time, or a trio, exclaim a match with glee and raise their hands. After a few more minutes, I could see numerous other individuals stop still in their search, close their eyes and mouths, raise their heads, and just listen. I, however, continued slogging away with my tone. I noticed I was having trouble staying with the note that I began with. I could sense some slippage or sliding. Slowly, I became aware that the overall sound of the room was changing. No longer was it a cacophony.

Within less than ten minutes, we were told to stop walking, continue to sing our notes, and listen to the total overall sound in the room. There were joyful expressions of awe! Remarkably, the sound in the room had changed from discord into a beautiful, rich, resonant chord that gained strength as we attended to it. It was an unexpected wonder.

Since that workshop, I have often associated that experience with the feeling that, over time, can come with praying. Praying with suffering has a loud crying out quality to it. It also doesn't sound pretty. It is an honest and true, unique expression of what we are feeling, and it is a limited version of who we are. We try to listen for a response. We try to become aware of a compassionate, resonant response that meets us where we are at.

The call-and-response of prayer is a relationship, a relationship in which Love is continually calling out to us to share our sound, and as we respond with our cry, we gradually become aware of and attune ourselves to Love accompanying us. This experience of attunement can feel like going from discord to a major chord, and it can happen fairly naturally, almost imperceptibly, until there is some felt transformation. We go from an individual alone to part of a whole that is bigger than us. We, as individuals, feel whole as we internally resonate, attune within ourselves, and feel our varied parts belong. Naturally, we feel grateful, and the resonance spreads.

Over the years, I tested out this analogy against my experience of prayer and suffering. While it naturally fit some people and situations of suffering, when it came to chronic suffering, it often was inadequate or failed. Our chronic suffering often doesn't blend in. Our notes we cry out don't slip. We don't unconsciously slide our discordant notes into an easy accord with others or Love or within ourselves. We can't. We hurt too much.

I corrected my original analogy. Imagine that, in the workshop exercise I just described, we are participating as chronic sufferers. Professional vocalists are trained to remain true to their notes and not lose them amidst the varied other sounds around them. Chronic sufferers have no choice. Though we wish otherwise, we are often limited to our one discordant repetitive expression. We can't unconsciously slide our expressions to blend in, and they don't just slip into accord with others.

We chronic sufferers do respond to the invitation to share our experience, our note. We can also become aware of what else is happening around us, and sure enough sometimes there is some resonance and matching of notes here and there in the ballroom of life. However, no sudden greater chord emerges from our group spontaneously. What does emerge among many of us is a desire to attune by finding different ways to connect and relate, and to become whole—within ourselves, with others, and with Love—even as we repetitively cry out. Slowly, we act creatively in ways that draw others into our efforts. We consciously search for the musical keys that groups of our varied notes fall within. Then we, too, form chords, less usual ones, not major chords, but minors, sevenths, and others. We alternate the expression of those chords in what turns out to be varying rhythms that can flow through the whole group in waves. Gradually, we feel we belong and are active, parts of whole new creations, new songs. We all, also, are grateful. The experience of being active parts of a whole spreads. All this is prayer, and to many of us it feels like love and Love.

IMAGINE AND PONDER

- We might try to blend in when we suffer in silence. Sometimes we are able to blend in when we and others know that our pain will eventually go away. Ongoing suffering often requires improvisation. Adjustments and accommodations form new ways of relating and may require new relationships.

Can we learn to appreciate new ways of accompanying each other as well as new songs with different rhythms and unexpected harmonies?

CHAPTER 21

BE AWARE

There is always more going on in our lives than suffering. The people who talk with us; the sun each day, whether or not it is behind clouds; the sounds of life, from birds chirping to leaf blowers; and the colors of our world—those are just a few of the external things. Internally, the particular ways our bodies still function well, our eyes or ears, for example, or our sense of touch; positive memories that come to us, pleasant ones from childhood or last week; our response to beauty in flowers, architecture, the patterns of clouds; plans for the next few hours; wishes for the far-off future; and our valuing something or someone important to us.

However, suffering narrows our focus, our perceptual bandwidth. Acute physical pain, emotional states like depression or anxiety, and interpersonal conflicts all limit what we perceive. Pain in one part of our body makes it difficult to notice someone caringly touching another part of our body. Anxiety about the future and hurt in the past interfere with realizing how safe and comfortable we are now. Being immersed in anger obstructs even hearing a sincere apology. These are facts. They are important because they suggest how we may not notice Love active in our lives.

Observing and noticing what else is occurring, what else is available to us, is a natural human capacity. However, faced with suffering, awareness often requires intention and effort. Intention and effort may not be available to us in acute discomfort. As natural as prayer is, we know there are days for some of us when even crying out is not possible. Experientially, we trust ourselves to do what we can do. When we are up for it, it is worth testing whether today we might be able to deepen our prayer. Who knows, today may be the day. If intention and effort for greater awareness are not available to us, and even if we can't cry out, Love continues to be with us compassionately. Love is working so that other people and happenstances will help us feel that love.

Becoming aware of what more there is in addition to our pain at least functions to distract us. The distraction of focusing on something else, even for brief seconds, can be a relief. Sometimes a less demanding way to become aware of more while suffering is through practicing a bit of distancing, or mindfulness. If we observe our pain over time, whether it be over minutes, hours, days, or years, we gradually become aware of how much our pain varies, in intensity, duration, and the felt experience of it (a dull ache or piercing, like crawling out of our skin or being ripped apart, emotionally like I want to die or mostly run away). Both distraction and distancing are practices of awareness that can decenter our pain, lessen our focus on it, and make room for other experiences and feelings, a greater experience of the whole of life.

There is still more, however, more than what comes with the natural capacities of distraction, distancing, and mindfulness. Everything more comes to us through relationship. Our natural capacities of awareness invite us to become actively conscious of relationship.

This particular awareness can transform the usual ground of our experience. The entire time we suffer, there is more, more coming to us and available through relationship. More of the whole of life is coming through relationship. Love is continually calling us and communicating to us through our relationships with all that is different and more than our suffering.

Reflect on this: the only ways that Love has to communicate with us are through our natural human capacities—our senses, our physical surroundings and experiences, our feelings, intelligence, dreams and daydreams, imaginations, creativity, and relationships. All are ways we experience the richness of others and the world. All are ways we can experience our relationship with Love. If Love is going to communicate directly or indirectly with us, the communication will come from within or without, always processed through our human capacities. What follows, then, is that if we want to hear more from Love, to feel closer or be more affected or held by Love, the more important it is to be open, observant, sensitive, and perceptive. The more aware we are of all there is, all there is in life, each other, the world, and the depths of ourselves, the more ways Love has of communicating and relating with us.

Isn't this the way it is in all good relationships? The better the friendship, the more ways we have of sharing, such as conversation, work, family experiences including family struggles, and joint activities from sports to shopping to cooking to eating to building something. In addition, the better the friendship, the greater the range of what we feel comfortable sharing: positive happenings as well as negative, feelings as well as thoughts as well as activities, desires and wishes as well as facts, and areas of confidence as well as challenges and doubt.

Especially when we are in some sort of pain, there is always more to perceive around us and view as part of our relationship with Love. The more can be in the details we take for granted or in what's new or different around us or within us. "Oh, look at that sunset." "Did you just see that hawk?" "How about that little flower, there on that weed that pushed up within the crack of the sidewalk?!" Often it is something beautiful or just surprising, often in nature, but it could just as well be something in humanity. "That person walking by just nodded and smiled at me!" It could be something happening with your own body. "I went outside for the first time in weeks, and I noticed the air on my skin." That is what my cousin Pete said after finally getting out of the hospital after weeks. These could all be seen as not just wonders in themselves, but gifts from Love that speak to us of the ongoing presence of Love in our lives.

To be aware of more is to shift the perspective of our stories of suffering. Something more and different feels possible because we can notice something other than pain, sense that something positive is actively in relationship with us. If our stories are like protected seeds planted in harsh conditions, to be aware is like those seeds sensing that there is water, the sun's warmth, or fertile soil available to degrees that were not previously imagined. It may be safe to germinate and then sprout after all, even in the midst of otherwise harsh conditions.

If our stories are like singing discordant notes, to be aware is to notice that others are actively with us, some of them suffering also. As they share their own notes, rather than repel each other, many are looking for ways to come together and relate more fully and positively even amidst their differences. There are positive possibilities even within discord—more lively rhythms, a range of other chords expressing a fuller sense of what's possible, a greater range of creativity, all kinds of music.

The difficulty with noticing more is that the most common elements of life exist alongside our suffering and do not take it away. Often, positive feelings only contrast with and don't contradict suffering. Positive relationships exist side by side with hurtful ones. In fact, any one relationship can be comforting in some ways and disturbing in others. We are challenged to practice being aware of, bearing, and even accepting multiple contrasting feelings and relationships at the same time.

I know this from my own experience. There was one day I remember well when Cousin Pete was in the hospital. It was very early spring, but the sun was out and the temperature was around seventy degrees. I ended up walking miles along a river to the hospital rather than driving on the freeway. I was aware and thankful for the sun, its warmth, the hope that comes with spring, and the chance to reflect as I walked instead of being focused on driving. It was a time for me to pray for Pete's health, my resilience and coping, and gratitude for supportive friends. I was thankful for some felt sense of Love's presence that had recently appeared in the marathon of challenges and suffering. I reminded Love to stay awake and with me.

However, to this day, I remember the acute disruptions to this positive scenario. As a pedestrian, I had to maneuver through a few major intersections across heavy traffic that pressed toward the major bridges crossing the river. As I managed the traffic lights, crosswalks, and traffic backups, I became acutely aware of the people in those cars and trucks who seemed barely aware of me as a pedestrian, let alone my suffering, and who did not give me a thought except perhaps in anger because I was in their way so they would have to slow down and be just a bit more cautious. I also was aware that this wonderful sun with its life-giving light and warmth was shining on those angry, pressured, unaware drivers as well as me—indiscriminately! So it was easy to feel angry and frustrated at the sun and Love. "Do you really care about me? About Pete? When you are blessing these insensitive, impatient people in their cars just as you are me?!" When suffering is close, it is so easy to feel even blessings are curses or signs of an uncaring, cold universe.

And this is when attunement comes in. When awareness may alert us to Love's presence but is not strong enough to let us be comforted by it, or when the comfort of Love's accompaniment is disrupted by our suffering, then active attunement can help.

IMAGINE AND PONDER

- Can we see and feel that we are in relationship with what more there is than our suffering? Can we perceive that we are being continually blessed and held with all good things through relationship with Love? Even in the midst of our suffering?

CHAPTER 22

ATTUNE

To be aware is different than to attune. To be aware is to change our focus and see from a different perspective. Rather than focus on our suffering, we widen our range of focus and notice what is more and other than suffering. We notice that we are in relationship with all those things and with their loving source. To attune, on the other hand, is not just to see but to intentionally further that perspective. We actively try to see through Love's eyes, and then we act intentionally in line with Love's vision. We try to participate in Love's vision, even partner with Love.

As I walked along the river to the hospital that day, as I crossed through the traffic, I oriented my perspective to Love being generous, accompanying everyone and everything, not just me. I questioned myself. Will I spurn what Love offered me because Love also offered to accompany someone else with the same warmth and light? I thought, just like those drivers don't know what is going on with me, whether or not I am hurting and how much, I have no idea which of them are also hurting and need the sun as much as I do, if not more. Maybe some of them are rushing their way to the same hospital.

Attunement is learning to see everything through Love's loving eyes. How does Love look upon me, what I do, how I relate? Not, for sure, as a judge standing apart, over and against me, but as one who sees me clearly, strengths and weaknesses, preoccupations and loves, and who all the while is in intimate caring relationship with me. Love knows me for who I really am, history and potential, all my varied parts, as well as how I live and love now. Love wants to know how I see myself, to compare notes with me, and then Love desires me to attune, to try treating myself in line with how Love sees me.

And always, there's more. Attunement also means that I, in turn, want to know more of Love. In fact, to attune is to gradually see and feel clearly and strongly that Love loves more than me and my inner circle of things and people. Love wants me to know, appreciate, and accompany all else that Love loves. Love wants and offers partnership and participation. Love wants me to see and engage you, all others, and our planet the way Love sees you all. That also would be me attuning to Love.

In regard to our prayer particularly, doesn't it make sense, then, that as part of Love's response to our intimately sharing our suffering, Love often places us in contact with aspects of our natural world and other people as well, the sunsets and people nodding hello. Love accompanies, appreciates, and holds everything close. We might see it all as gift. Some of these could be comforting to us. Again, I know that, in our pain, we may not be able to perceive or appreciate many of them. Also, in an evolving, incomplete world with incomplete, evolving humans, I don't doubt that some events, things, or people that come our way will not be gifts but instead will bring more hurt. Stay away from or stand against those—being attuned with Love also includes identifying and actively moving away from or standing against what is closed to or works against Love. Nevertheless, some gifts can be happily shared with others, and Love could be introducing us to others so that we can bring Love to them and somehow comfort their suffering—yes, maybe even as we ourselves continue to suffer. So, part of Love's response to our praying with suffering could be to put us in contact with someone else who also is suffering and who we can share Love with.

I was in my fifties when Cousin Pete was in the hospital. It was a dark period for me. I was focused on trying my best to care for Pete and overcoming my inadequacies as a caregiver. I doubted I was a good shepherd. I doubted I was affectively caring for my sheep. Then, unexpectedly, I was aware of new people in my life and the possibility of getting to know them. I didn't think of them as gifts. In fact, at first, I felt guilty that I wasn't focusing every free moment on Cousin Pete, and I felt I had nothing to offer these people in return for their interest and support—it seemed to me that all I was doing was caring for Pete and working full-time. It would have been easy to turn away from engaging new people. I didn't turn away, however, and gradually we became good close friends. I accepted that I needed some different additional sources of support and healing. Slowly I realized I needed more, and I gradually saw that I was giving something back to these people who were so present to me in my darkness. Fifteen years later, a number of them are still with me, sharing mutual friendship.

My life was changed in a fundamental and surprising way and blessed in that dark period, transformed. I am grateful for those friends. I am also grateful that I had the capacities to stay open, perceive, receive, and appreciate and care for them in return, all in the midst of my suffering and the suffering of my cousin. I am grateful that I attuned to Love.

IMAGINE AND PONDER

- Can we imagine that Love is inviting us, when we are able, to respond with love to others' pain even as we are immersed in our own?

CHAPTER 23

BE GRATEFUL

When we become aware of what more there is than our suffering, what more there is available and being given to us in relationship, then we are receiving gifts. Of course, our natural response is to be grateful. When we begin to attune ourselves to a life force so generous that we naturally want to participate with it, then we are actively grateful. These are the moments when joy enters. Love feels good to receive, but joy comes as love is acknowledged and passed on, shared.

The easiest and most natural way to acknowledge and pass love on is to be thankful. One way to attune to Love's active relationship in our lives is through gratitude. We can express thanks for what more, beyond suffering, Love has gifted us and for our relationship with Love. Giving thanks is a way to be joyful and a way to respond to, attune to, and share Love's spirit. We can be thankful for whatever opportunities Love has put before us in the midst of our pain. From the perspective of call-and-response, our most natural and fundamental response to love and Love in our lives is to be grateful.

It can be difficult to feel thankful in the midst of suffering. Don't worry if you don't feel it. Trust yourself and your feelings, or your lack of them. As we've practiced throughout this book, everything can be shared in relationship, and doing so contributes to the intimacy of the relationship. So, it is possible to say, while looking Love in the eyes, "Love, I don't feel thankful to you. I am not grateful," and see Love look at you with understanding, acceptance, and compassion. You just might see Love or Jesus look at you appreciatively, for your willingness to share, your honesty, your courage, maybe just your vulnerable presence.

At any point in the interplay of call-and-response that is the relationship of prayer, you might feel gratitude for any interaction or any aspect of the relationship you become aware of. You might be thankful for being called to express yourself, or for becoming aware of particular responses in nature or other people. It is important to be on the lookout for the response of gratitude within you, even a faint and tentative thank you. Whenever you do feel it, express it as part of your prayer. Love leads to more love; gratitude leads to more to be grateful for. Like love, thankfulness is gradually and powerfully transformative.

IMAGINE AND PONDER

- Can we imagine that saying "Thanks" in prayer or to a person or to some aspect of the universe is a way of both responding to the gifts of Love and passing the joy of love on? Test it out.

CONCLUSION

Over forty years ago, I transformed a Gospel story for the first time for someone I cared about. As I shared here, during the ensuing years and continuing into the present, I have prayed with my own suffering. I have transformed Gospel stories to fit my experience and relationship with Love. I have prayed for others' suffering as well, both those I know and care about and people I don't know personally but have only heard about. For those people, I have transformed many Gospel stories and prayed with those stories, often over and over.

Looking back, only now do I see that suffering with Love has been fundamental to my life. Fortunately, there also has been much to be grateful for and much joy.

My favorite Christian Gospel story is the disciples walking to Emmaus after Jesus was tortured to death. That story holds so much of what I have tried to pass on in this book.

I imagine those two disciples as they walk to Emmaus are not only frightened, confused, and disheartened. I imagine they are traumatized by the violence poured out on someone they love and deeply depressed by how another good and loving person could be so unjustly destroyed by the oppressive society they live in. Then another person appears and walks with them. They don't recognize him as Jesus or as Love. They don't recognize him until, in the midst of sharing their suffering, he breaks the bread they have, blesses it, and offers it to them. They don't recognize him until, while sharing suffering, they also share and are nourished by love. They don't recognize Love until they share suffering and love.

It's a story of how we recognize Love in the midst of our brokenness and our suffering, both ours and Love's. It's also a story of how, in the midst of shared suffering, we nourish and nurture each other. It's a story of sharing love. We share Love by loving.

Jesus chose bread as central to the two greatest prayers we have from him. In one he said, "Give us, this day, our daily bread." The words of the other have become the consecration for the Eucharist: "He took bread," chose, broke, blessed, and gave it.

How we recognize ourselves, each other, and Love in bread, is at first through our shared vulnerability, our hunger and longing, our brokenness, our suffering. Then, attuning ourselves to Love, our response is to know that each of us still is chosen and loved—suffering and being broken should not separate us. In fact, we share bread in the midst of being broken, take and give ourselves to each other in the midst of suffering, and compassionately nurture and nourish each other. We love and sustain each other each day as we are loved and sustained by Love each day. There's so much to be grateful for.

We can't separate love and Love.

Prayer heals the way love heals.

PS: As you test out the visions of prayer and love in this book, let me know your experiences. Email me at tim@forcryingoutlove.com.

EPILOGUE

Beginning in the introduction, stories related to my mother are scattered throughout this book. That's not a coincidence. I wrote this book that is so focused on suffering during my mother's long, almost four-year, final journey. What is a coincidence or synchronicity is that she died the day I sent the just-completed manuscript to a compassionate copyeditor.

My mother was in hospice for the last year of her life, and I was managing most of her twenty-four-hour in-home care during that period from a distance. While my goal over these last years was to have her die peacefully and without pain, that is not something any of us have complete control over. Fortunately, she did die peacefully and without pain. She was held by love in the heart of Love. She was with people who cared deeply for her. On the day she died, one of those people held a phone near her ear, and my mother heard me tell her I loved her, that I hoped she could relax into the love that surrounded her and held her, and that we would be OK. I was told a tear came to her eye as I spoke. Tears wet my eyes too.

I have come to believe the most profound ongoing conflict we humans face in our lives is between how much we continue to strive to be and possess, and how much we accept our limitations and what we have already. At any age and in most situations, the tension between striving and accepting is challenging. I don't think it is ever a black-and-white dichotomy. It is a tension that is most obvious when suffering. How much do we try for more healing, a fuller life, and ask more of ourselves and others, and how much do we test out accepting and appreciating what we have now? There is so much unknown in these questions. We never know if the results of striving will be worth our efforts. Often, we don't even know if our efforts will cause more suffering rather than less. And certainly, we never know what might have been if...

I wrote this book knowing the difficulties of long-term suffering from personal experiences in my own life and my experiences working in psychotherapy with people I cared deeply about. I wrote it immersed in the suffering of my mother and family as my mother declined and died. I wrote it wanting the familiar Christian Gospel stories to better reflect my experience and that of the others in my life. And I wrote it wanting to help us all feel how we are held by Love and called by Love to relationship with Love in every moment, even in our most difficult moments.

My experience is that the most profound and useful thing that we can strive for more of in our lives is love, and the most profound and useful thing we can accept and appreciate now is love. While often challenging, I believe this was my mother's experience as well. Maybe you will find this to be true for you and those you care about.

ACKNOWLEDGMENTS

Is there anything more valuable than friends and the graced relationships with other open and generous people who contribute to our life paths? I can't imagine what.

The content of this book began to sprout over four decades ago. Even then there were many people who had already helped to till the ground, plant the seeds, and nourish the roots as they developed. Oh, and they did their best to help me identify and control the weeds that are part of any challenging life and its projects.

Now you hold and are reading the fruit of many people's gifts and labor with me. I am so thankful for all who have contributed, and I take responsibility for any flaws.

I thank especially those who worked with me in psychotherapy, who shared the intimacies and efforts of their lives with me. My relationships with you as well as my relationship with my beloved Pam challenged and strengthened everything that developed into this book.

For those who read drafts of chapters and those who just expressed interest in and support for my efforts and the ideas and values here, I am grateful. You are among my good friends.

Finally, I know that Love continually holds all and holds us close as we try to hold each other.

I thank Love.

MEET THE AUTHOR

I am grateful for the over forty years I spent working in psychotherapy with adult individuals and couples. Before retiring as a clinical psychologist, I practiced and taught psychoanalysis and psychoanalytic psychotherapy. Among other institutions, I served on the faculty of the Boston Psychoanalytic Society and Institute, and for twenty-five years I was on the clinical faculty of Harvard Medical School. I utilized Internal Family Systems, and I companioned people in spiritual direction. In addition to a PhD in clinical psychology, I earned a pastoral ministry certificate from Boston College. My undergraduate degree is from the University of Notre Dame.

I live outside Boston, Massachusetts, with my beloved, Pam, with whom I share all that life brings.

Currently, I'm being called to reflect and write in a variety of experience-near creative ways on two profound human experiences. One is how difficult it is to distinguish Love (a.k.a. God or the Ultimate Mystery) from love. The other is one of our most continual life conflicts: How much do we strive to develop and flourish (even pray to do so), and how much do we accept and appreciate our limitations. Of course, this isn't a black-or-white dichotomy. Everyone has strengths to develop and limitations to adjust to. However, as I learned throughout my career and personal life, this conflict is most obvious when we ourselves, or those we care about, have chronic or recurrent challenges that bring suffering. That suffering could be from relationship difficulties, being immersed in the consequences of trauma, drug addiction, emotional illness, and/or physical illness and death.

For Crying Out Love is a result of engaging both of these profound human experiences. I am focused on the recurring suffering in our lives, the love we give and receive, and Love that holds and companions all.

www.ingramcontent.com/pod-product-compliance
Ingram Content Group UK Ltd.
Pitfield, Milton Keynes, MK11 3LW, UK
UKHW041630190726
13854UKWH00006B/2397